Growing Into Soul:

The Next Step in Human Evolution

A Practical Guide to Living Wisely and Well
in the 21st Century

Gwen Randall-Young

TRAFFORD

© Copyright 2004 Gwen Randall-Young. All rights reserved.

No part of this publication may be reproduced, stored in a retrieval system, or transmitted, in any form or by any means, electronic, mechanical, photocopying, recording, or otherwise, without the written prior permission of the author.

Printed in Victoria, Canada

Cover Design: Gwen Randall-Young
Cover Photo: Tasha Young

A cataloguing record for this book that includes the U.S. Library of Congress Classification number, the Library of Congress Call number and the Dewey Decimal cataloguing code is available from the National Library of Canada. The complete cataloguing record can be obtained from the National Library's online database at: www.nlc-bnc.ca/amicus/index-e.html
ISBN: 1-41250-1404-2

Gwen Randall-Young
**439 Village Drive
Sherwood Park, AB, CANADA
T8A 4K1**

TRAFFORD

This book was published *on-demand* **in cooperation with Trafford Publishing.** On-demand publishing is a unique process and service of making a book available for retail sale to the public taking advantage of on-demand manufacturing and Internet marketing. **On-demand publishing** includes promotions, retail sales, manufacturing, order fulfilment, accounting and collecting royalties on behalf of the author.

Suite 6E, 2333 Government St., Victoria, B.C. V8T 4P4, CANADA
Phone   250-383-6864   Toll-free   1-888-232-4444 (Canada & US)
Fax   250-383-6804   E-mail   sales@trafford.com
Web site   www.trafford.com   TRAFFORD PUBLISHING IS A DIVISION OF TRAFFORD HOLDINGS LTD.
Trafford Catalogue #03-1782   www.trafford.com/robots/03-1782.html

10   9   8   7   6

OTHER BOOKS AND AUDIOTAPES
by
Gwen Randall-Young

Dancing Soul: The Voice of Spirit Evolving

Baby Soul: A Blessing of Spirit

Echoes Through Time: A Message of Healing for Men

Healing the Past: A Meditation for Wholeness (on audiotape).

A World of Kindness: Experiencing Personal and Global Harmony (on audiotape)

For more writing by the author, to contact her, or to order books, please visit:

www.gwen.ca

Soul is that unmistakable fire that infuses all truly creative endeavors and sends the shiver up the spine, telling us we're in the presence of *lived truth*.
> *Phil Cousineau*

The soul is a breath of living spirit,
that with sensitivity,
permeates the entire body to give it life.
> *Hildegard of Bingen*

The soul looketh steadily forwards, creating a world before her, leaving worlds behind her. She has no dates, nor rites, nor persons, nor specialties nor men. The soul knows only the soul; the web of events is the flowing robe in which she is clothed.
> *Ralph Waldo Emerson*

The breeze at dawn has secrets to tell you,
    Don't go back to sleep.
You must ask for what you really want.
    Don't go back to sleep.
People are going back and forth across the doorsill
    where two worlds touch.
The door is round and open,
    Don't go back to sleep.
> *Jelaluddin Rumi*

CONTENTS

PREFACE ix
INTRODUCTION 1
    GROWING TOGETHER 2

1 **EGO AND SOUL** 7
    CHOICE 9
    WHAT IS EGO? WHAT IS SOUL? 10
    HOW DOES EGO DEVELOP? 12
    WHAT THEN, IS SOUL? 19
    THE EMERGENCE OF SOUL 24
    THE VOICES OF EGO AND SOUL 26
    WHEN EGO DIRECTS LIFE 27
    SOUL DIRECTED LIFE 29
    THE LINK TO SPIRITUALITY 31

2 **SCIENCE CONNECTS BODY, MIND AND SOUL** 37
    EMOTIONS AND THE IMMUNE SYSTEM 37
    STRESS AND DISTRESS 39
    HEALING 41
    SOUL AND HEALING 43
    THE ROLE OF SOUL IN HUMAN EVOLUTION 45
    HEART AND SOUL 51
    IMPLICATIONS 53

3 **THE CONTINUUM OF AWARENESS AND BEHAVOR** 55
    EGO 'THINKING AND SOUL 'KNOWING' 55
    UNDERSTANDING 60

	COMPASSION	62
	ACCEPTANCE	65
	AS WE INTERPRET, SO WE CREATE	67

4 PREPARATION FOR THE JOURNEY ... 72
  GETTING READY FOR CHANGE ... 72
  TWO BASIC PRINCIPLES ... 74
  OF WHAT SIGNIFICANCE ARE PAST EXPERIENCES? ... 75
  EXPANDING PERCEPTION: WE ARE MOVING TOWARDS THE LIGHT ... 77
  LIVING A PARADOX: WE ARE PREPROGRAMMED,
    AND WE ARE THE CREATORS OF OUR OWN LIVES ... 78
  THE PROCESS OF EXPANDING AWARENESS
    CAN BE ENHANCED ... 81
  IF IT IS SO SIMPLE, WHY IS LIFE A STRUGGLE? ... 83

5 MOVING FORWARD–RELEASING THE OLD ... 85
  POLARITY ... 85
  AGGRESSION ... 86
  ANGER ... 86
  FEAR ... 87
  THE NEED TO BE RIGHT ... 88
  THE NEED TO CONTROL ... 89
  DENIAL ... 90
  FALSE SELF ... 91
  IF I LET GO, WHO WILL I BE? ... 93
  ACCESSING TRUE SELF ... 94

6 LOVE: A SOULFUL PERSPECTIVE ... 97
  THE FORCE THAT CONNECTS ... 97
  EGO, SOUL AND LIFE FORCE ... 98
  CHILDHOOD EXPERIENCES OF LOVE ... 99
  ADOLESCENT IDEAS ABOUT LOVE ... 100
  LOVE AS NEED ... 100
  CONDITIONAL LOVE IN MARRIAGE ... 101
  CONTROLLING LOVE ... 103
  SOULFUL LOVING ... 104
  EXERCISES ... 105

7	**LOVE IN FAMILIES**	106
	PARENTS AND CHILDREN	106
	CONDITIONAL LOVE	108
	UNCONDITIONAL LOVE	110
	THE REPORT CARD	112
	MISBEHAVIOR	114
	COMMON SENSE	115
	TEENAGERS	116
	A TWIST IN THE PLOT	119
	EVOLUTIONARY RESPONSIBILITY	122
	EXERCISES	122
	ADULT FAMILIES	123
	PARENTS	124
	ABUSIVE PARENTS	126
	ADULT SIBLINGS	128
	SOUL SIBLINGS	130
	CONCLUSION	132
	EXERCISES	133
8	**LOVE IN INTIMATE RELATIONSHIP**	134
	COURTSHIP	135
	THE HONEYMOON IS OVER	137
	BECOMING OUR PARENTS	138
	SOULFUL LOVING	139
	EGO AND SOUL IN RELATIONSHIP	141
	WENDY AND DAVE	142
	SERENA AND ALI	146
	JOE AND GLORIA	150
	MAKING THE SHIFT	154
	CHOICE	155
	LETTING GO	157
	TAKING THE LEARNING	159
	EXERCISES	161
9	**EGO AND SOUL AT WORK**	162
	CONTINUUM OF CONSCIOUSNESS AT WORK	163
	WORK AS A CONTEXT FOR EXPRESSING OUR HUMANESS	167
	MAKING ALL WORK SOULFUL	169

	EXERCISES	173
10	**BRINGING IT ALL HOME**	174
	A MATTER OF MONEY	176
	WHAT IS THE TEACHER TEACHING?	177
	AN ISSUE OF TRUST	178
	A LITTLE WHITE LIE	179
	OOPS, I FORGOT	180
	YOU CAN'T SAY THAT TO ME	181
	MARRIAGE BREAKDOWN	183
	DOWNSIZED	185
	SOUL-BASED LIVING	187
	EXERCISES	189
11	**THE ULTIMATE LETTING GO**	190
	DEATH: NEMESIS OR TEACHER?	190
	IMPERMANENCE	194
	TRANSCENDING EGO	197
	PHYSICAL DEATH	200
	METAMORPHOSIS	202
	EXERCISES:	202
12	**FULL CIRCLE**	204
	SOUL'S EXPERIENCE ON EARTH	205
	SOUL TAKES FLIGHT	205
	CONSCIOUS EVOLUTION	207
	GROWING INTO SOUL: THE NEXT STEP IN HUMAN EVOLUTION	211

Preface

Almost thirty years ago Jonas Salk wrote a book called *Survival of the Wisest,* in which he argued that in order for the human species to survive and thrive in the second half of its growth curve, there would have to be a shift in values and perspectives. Wisdom would overtake physical strength as the primary predictor of evolutionary endurance, for both the individual and the species. This would mark a major evolutionary shift.

That shift has begun, and its tremors will touch us all. Findings of quantum physics suggest a cosmic intelligence at the core of the Universe: the substrate from which all else manifests. Through human consciousness, the Universe can reflect upon itself for the first time. Each individual has access to pure perception (insight), but, according to physicist David Bohm, our low level of ego development deflects that insight.

What is required to access this insight, or wisdom, is the ability to transcend our own egos. Only then may we tap into, and become expressions of that underlying order which exists everywhere, including within our own DNA.

Cosmic intelligence is the energy that pulsates through the outer regions of the universe, and the inner reaches of individual consciousness. Its human expression is soul.

The goal of this quest is no longer simply esoteric 'enlightenment'. Modern science demonstrates the impact of our thoughts on every level of physical and mental health. Simply put, ego-based thoughts and behaviors are ultimately detrimental. The negative effects extend to physical health, interpersonal relationships, and consequently, individual and collective wellbeing.

Science is revealing startling evidence of the effects of a more soul-based perspective at the level of cells, bio-chemicals and electrical impulses within the body. Thoughts and behaviors aligned with soul contribute positively to health and happiness, consequently, they are 'pro-evolutionary'.

Growing Into Soul: The Next Step in Human Evolution is a guide to assist humans in navigating this evolutionary transition. There has recently been a great shift towards an awareness of the collective consciousness—millions are seeking to appease their spiritual hunger and connect with soul.

While many are becoming increasingly familiar with these spiritual ideas on a conceptual level, they still struggle to integrate them into 'real life': applying them consistently in day-to-day living. Making the shift is difficult.

As David Bohm says, the collectivity does not yet have "the energy to reach the whole, to put it all on fire". The purpose of this book is to ignite within every reader the energy and intelligence to make this evolutionary shift.

Growing Into Soul: The Next Step in Human Evolution is written simply and clearly, so that the concepts are accessible to a wide variety of readers. It begins by developing the concepts of ego and soul, and providing scientific evidence for the pro-evolutionary benefits of soulful living.

The practical application is demonstrated through a proposed continuum of awareness and behavior, from ego to soul-based perceptions. This revolutionary idea emphasizes the human capacity to choose how one perceives life experiences. Concrete explanations and examples are provided to facilitate the release of the old ego dominated ways of being.

The process outlined in the first half of the book is then applied to daily living with chapters devoted to relationship, families, the workplace, and death, as ego's final challenge. Each chapter ends with a few exercises allowing the reader to integrate the learning. A diagram is also provided, illustrating the emotions, behaviors, and characteristics of life that flow from consciously accessing soul's wisdom, as opposed to reacting on the basis of ego interpretations.

The practical wisdom outlined in this book emerges out of the author's professional experience successfully assisting thousands to apply these principles in their everyday lives. What is unique about the book is the way in which sophisticated concepts are simplified, and applied to situations we all encounter. This is what so many have been seeking: a realistic and practical manual for integrating body, mind and soul; a guide for creating health and happiness. Now, it is in your hands. Let the journey begin.

Introduction

The deepest question in the heart of humans throughout time has yet to be answered: "Who am I?" There are theories, stories, myths, beliefs, and spiritual traditions in every tribe, culture and language, and in every geographical region of our world. Despite all of these, every generation brings a new wave of seekers and searchers, embracing some of the old, and creating their own new theories. We do not need theories or myths to explain why it gets dark at night, why seasons change, or why, sometimes, the sun or moon is eclipsed. We *know*. Why is it taking so long to figure out who we are and why we are here?

At any stage in development of the individual or the species as a whole, our understanding is only as good as the knowledge and tools we possess. As these become more refined, our understanding grows deeper, and more accurate.

Cosmologists have suggested it is only through human consciousness that the Universe can be 'aware' of itself. Primitive man had a consciousness somewhat like that of an infant. With no language, he was controlled by impulses and drives: unaware of the world beyond his direct perceptions.

As humans have evolved, so too has consciousness. As we have 'grown up', we have come to understand more of the world and the cosmos, but also more about ourselves.

As a species, we are on the verge of a great awakening. For the first time in human history, we are arriving at a point where we are beginning to grasp a bigger picture of who we are, and how we fit in this magnificent universe.

It has taken the combined wisdom of the ancient traditions, the spiritual understandings of all of the earth's peoples, the brilliant minds of philosophers and poets, along with the sophisticated advances of modern science to bring us to this point. The pieces are starting to come together. Not only do they reveal answers to age-old questions, but they point in the direction of a new way of being. Like an unfolding treasure hunt, we now have enough information and a sufficiently developed consciousness to propel ourselves towards the next evolutionary shift.

Contained within the human embryo is all the information required to become a mature adult. Similarly, the seeds of the evolutionary maturation of our species were planted eons ago. We have passed through the infancy and childhood of our species. We have been in the adolescent stage for a time. Now, we are poised for independent adulthood.

For the first time ever, we can consciously participate in our own evolution. On the threshold of realizing untapped human capabilities, we are now in a position to create and direct our future, both as individuals, and as a species.

GROWING TOGETHER

Humans need each other in order to grow. Children raised in isolated conditions do not develop beyond a primitive level. Through our lives, our growth is a product of the interaction of our own consciousness with that of others. There is also a 'collective consciousness' existing at the level of community, be that tribal, local or national, as well as a global consciousness.

Relationship with others is the context in which we grow and learn. The qualities that characterize our individual consciousness, are reflected in our relationships. The qualities that characterize our social consciousness are reflected in world events. We exist within an interconnected human web. What we do individually has an impact on the whole, and what happens to the whole, impacts individual consciousness.

The challenges we face personally and globally provide the raw materials, as well as the mirrors, for the development of our consciousness. We all have the ability to access deep inner wisdom, and to operate from a higher level of consciousness. To the extent we do that, life is more balanced, peaceful and satisfying. Where there is conflict, pain, animosity, estrangement, and struggle, we can be sure access to that deep wisdom is blocked.

There is no shortage of wisdom in the world. Much has been written both in ancient and modern times. Spiritual traditions embody principles that could lead to a far more peaceful, enlightened civilization. With television and the Internet, there is instant access to a plethora of 'how-to' and self-help information that infiltrates both individual and mass consciousness. Why then, can we not live according to these eternal truths that have been expressed since man developed the ability to communicate? Why can we understand them, yet be unable to apply them consistently in the practical world of our daily life?

Children evolve into more compassionate, responsible beings through a process of being exposed to principles, and then having life experiences which *challenge* them to overcome their initial impulses. Ideally, they have parents who guide them, and provide consequences for aggressive, selfish, or inappropriate responses. Children learn to *transcend* their automatic, knee-jerk responses. As adults, the process is much more subtle. The consequences are much more subtle.

The shift to responsible awareness and the understanding that we co-create all of the consequences existing in our lives is just beginning to emerge. For those who begin to grasp this concept, there is still confusion about how to *live it*, especially in a world where so many are not!

What is needed now is some concrete, practical direction. If young children can be taught to use computers, there must be a way of teaching a *technology of change* that anyone can understand and implement almost instantly.

What is needed is a bridge connecting the practical demands of living and the higher principles or wisdom. This book offers that possibility. It provides guiding principles whose implementation automatically honors the higher spiritual qualities, whether or not they are completely understood. It allows you, the reader, to create positive change in your life, regardless of how many books you have read, seminars you have attended, or whether or not you know how to meditate.

You will learn about the higher wisdom of the soul, and how to distinguish it from ego-driven feelings and behavior. You will be introduced to the *continuum of human behaviors* along which we progress on our path to healthy, harmonious lives. Convincing evidence from scientific research will show that thoughts, moods, emotions and belief systems have a profound impact on basic health and healing mechanisms of the body. You will see how thoughts and feelings can contribute to illness, or *reverse it*.

Survival of the human species depends on our ability to change the way we respond and react to life situations. This book will assist you in bringing all aspects of your life into alignment with soul—that aspect of our being which houses the knowing designed to carry us to the next level of human evolution. When thoughts, feelings and behaviors are in alignment with the most soulful aspects of our being, life becomes peaceful, centered, effortless, and even joyful.

Chapter One will take you directly to an understanding of what is meant by the terms 'ego' and 'soul'. You will learn how to recognize these aspects within yourself, and why this knowledge is crucial to both your own future, and the future of our species.

Chapter 1

EGO AND SOUL

As a psychotherapist, I can close my eyes and envision the hundreds, if not thousands of clients who have walked through my office doors. They come from all walks of life, representing a wide variety of income levels, ages, educational levels, cultural groups, and spiritual or non-spiritual orientations. They are all looking for the same thing.

Regardless of the symptoms or concerns they bring, each one is struggling to find something that seems just out of reach. The presenting problem they bring is only a symptom. While it may appear they are searching for a solution to an *external* problem, always, it seems to me, they are looking for an *inner* solution.

They may not know what they are looking for, or where to find it, but it is as clear to me as if I were watching someone stumble around in the dark looking for a light switch. They may not be ready to find what they are looking for, or to recognize it when they see it, but they are reaching around for it in the same way that a newborn roots around to find the breast of its mother.

Anxiety, depression, low self-esteem, difficulty in relationships, and even job dissatisfaction have at their core the struggle between who one is inside, and who one is expected to be, by self or others, in the world. These human struggles may be disharmonious vibrations, which occur, like the shaking of a vehicle, when something is out of alignment.

There is an instinctive, built-in drive in the direction towards wholeness. Sometimes the path to wholeness seems anything but: more often, it feels like everything is falling apart.

Something *is* falling apart, but, like the crumbling shell of a newborn chick, it falls apart so we may enter a much larger realm of experience. Imagine little chick eggs lining up outside of the 'poultry therapist's' office. Some report that they feel fragile; others think they are cracking up. Still others come in clutching all the shattered bits of shell in hopes that the therapist can help put them back together so everything will be okay again.

The therapist who tries to do that is not helping at all. This would only prolong the pain, for the chick would spend the rest of his or her life trying desperately to 'keep it all together'. Even if a way were found to hold it together, growth would be stunted, the natural process of life sabotaged, and the little chick would remain in darkness.

What is it then, for which humans are reaching? What is this inner drive that pulls us forward, not to Nirvana, but right into the heart of life's struggles? *It is the whispering of our own soul.* Just as the newborn carries, within, the memory of its Mother's beating heart, so we each carry, within, the memory of our soul essence, our soul's vibration, and our soul's purpose.

But why the struggle? Why not just begin moving to the rhythm of our own souls? This might be like asking why the first sea creatures to leave the ocean took so long to evolve. A new stage in human evolution is unfolding now, so there will be the same effort that always accompanies birth, be it the birth of a child or a galaxy.

The human soul is wrapped in the cocoon of ego. It cannot simply take flight any more than the butterfly can skip the stage of working its way out of the cocoon that protected it in its earlier form. Not recognizing that we are evolving into something more elegant than before, we hold tightly to ego believing it is all we have. Therein lies the struggle. Soul is pushing to be free, while ego tightens its grip. If it feels like we are stuck sometimes, it is because we are. Held there in the dynamic of opposing forces, we feel immobilized, frustrated, and disheartened. Not understanding what is happening within, we look outside of ourselves for the cause of our distress.

CHOICE

The central thesis of this book is that we are at a point in our development as humans where we must make a shift from a self-centered perspective, to a broader, more encompassing one. I am reminded of the early days of television when every set had a pair of 'rabbit ear' antennae sitting on the top of its wooden surface. At that time, we had two channels from which to choose. With cable or a satellite dish, there are now hundreds of channels available. The less evolved ego-based personality has only a few available responses, which are often reactions to something outside of itself. The personality that can access soul-knowing has endless possibilities.

We are *evolving* as a species, and the defining moment in moving to the next stage in our individual evolution is the recognition that we can *choose* how we are going to interpret what we perceive. Further, we can choose from options that are at a completely different level than the old, polarized, limited-channel options. How we choose to perceive, or the channels to which we tune ourselves, will determine the quality of our life's programming. We are born with the necessary technology, but if we do not know that, we fail to hook it up.

If we allow ourselves to 'tune in' to the higher levels of consciousness, we transform ourselves into more evolved beings. Once we have this insight, our perceptions and behaviors can become conscious, inner-directed, and purposeful. It is like having a map in unfamiliar territory. We can chart a course without fear of becoming lost. Without this insight, perceptions and responses remain unconscious reactions to our world. We are without either a map, or a sense of direction, and so may end up hopelessly lost, somewhere that is not of our choosing, or going around in circles.

For the purposes of this book, the narrower, reactive, unconscious perspective will be characterized as ego. The broader, all-knowing responsive perspective will be characterized as soul. It is important to note that ego is not bad, and the goal is not to get rid of ego altogether. It is about expanding the options available to us as human beings, so that we may actively, co-creatively, and elegantly participate in our own evolution.

It will be shown that this is an evolution towards a more soulful way of being: an alignment with the Spirit or Oneness, which pervades and includes everything, including us. Only when ego has been tamed, however, is the soul free to emerge into full consciousness within us.

WHAT IS EGO? WHAT IS SOUL?

Ego and soul are words that are used freely both by writers, and in our everyday conversations. So familiar are these terms, it is easy to assume ego and soul are concrete aspects of humans. It is more correct to say they are concepts: words used to describe aspects of humans. No kind of surgery or sophisticated technology will reveal or isolate the part of a person that is ego or soul. Language is limited, being a product of the human mind. Every language has some phrases that cannot be expressed accurately in another language; the same meaning cannot be captured. Similarly, there are some aspects of experience that cannot be expressed in words. Zen philosophers refer to 'that which cannot be named'. Language cannot possibly name all that is: new words are constantly evolving to attempt to describe emerging human experiences. Scientists might suggest if something cannot be isolated, seen or quantified, then it cannot exist. The truth is our lives are filled with things that cannot be defined in scientific terms, yet their existence is real for us. Love is one. Ambience, beauty, and intuition are others.

Ego and soul are words, which we have used to try to name and differentiate aspects of the human perception and behavior. Throughout this book, they will at times be used as descriptive words, and other times they will be described as though they are real, concrete entities. This is not the case: they are aspects of a human self, which is not a static structure either, but rather a living process. What is significant is not whether ego or soul exist, but rather, what it is we are trying to communicate in using these words. As always, what is most powerful is the unseen, the unknowable. The head uses words to describe, or to talk around what the heart knows is there. The following descriptions will give you a feel for the difference, so you may begin to conceptualize these terms in relation to your own life experience.

The word ego has been used in various contexts throughout history. It has been defined as the part of self that is conscious of itself, different from the subconscious. It has also been used to denote disproportionately valuing oneself over others, as in "egotistical" or having a big ego, which is not how it will be used here. In the context of this book, ego refers simply to the self, the three-dimensional thinking self: to who it is we *think* we are. Ego is the sum total of what we believe about ourselves, based on how others have responded to us throughout life, how we see ourselves in society, and our emotional reactions to our experiences. Ego experiences things in relation to itself. Ego is the sun, everything else, the planets, stars, or empty space. This does not refer to the importance ego places upon itself, only to its perspective.

HOW DOES EGO DEVELOP?

If you have ever held a newborn, you will know the powerful energy surrounding that tiny being. I was privileged to be present at the birth of my godchild, Grace, and held her minutes after her birth. While I had given birth to three of my own children, and marveled at each one, it is a completely different experience to watch another woman's child enter the world. It is not your baby, yet the feelings of the overwhelming miracle of it all are equally, if not more profound.

When you give birth to your own, you have been carrying the child for nine months, been in labor for some time, and feel relief when the child is born. Hormones are surging through your body: so much is happening all at once. It takes a while for it all to sink in. When you are an objective observer, the mind is totally clear; in fact, I felt a heightened awareness. To see a tiny being emerge from the Mother's womb and take its first breath is a most awe-inspiring event.

What I felt in that moment was a profound compassion for every one of us who has made that journey into the light of the world. I saw the perfection of the physical form that evolved from one tiny fertilized egg. I was overwhelmed by the vulnerability and complete dependence of the human infant. Most of all, I was astounded by the way in which the energy of that tiny being filled and transformed the room. I knew I was experiencing pure soul, unmediated by thought, by ego, or by earthly experience. I wept as I realized *we all start out that way, but then have to work to regain our connection to the soulfulness that once infused every cell of our being.* Some never do.

Imagine seeing someone with a state-of-the-art computer, who thinks it is simply a typewriter with a screen. We might groan when we think of the untapped potential in that computer. That potential will never be realized if the user has limited beliefs about the computer's capability.

Because babies cannot talk, people assume they are blank slates. If you look into the eyes of even a very young child, you can *feel* that child communicating with you. Sadly, by the time children have words to express themselves, the memory of their soulful existence has been programmed out of them. Too often, they become like the computer printer, simply putting out what has been 'typed' onto their consciousness.

Even in the most subtle ways, parents begin to 'shape' their child into the vision they hold of who he or she should grow up to be. I have heard parents of a six-month old say, " I am not going to have a child who behaves like that!" referring to the behavior of a one-year old that is typical for his age. Once an acquaintance told me that when her kindergarten child came downstairs dressed for school in a creative ensemble of her own choosing, she marched her back upstairs to change saying, "No child of mine will go out of the house looking like that!"

At a very early age, natural expressions of individuality are curtailed. Children learn that love and approval flow most abundantly when adults are pleased. They learn to begin to deny their own essences: even to feel that their inner urges, guidance, curiosity, and perceptions are wrong or bad. Often, this means suppressing what is naturally joyful, and going for what is pleasing to others instead. In time, they may forget how to even access the organic joy that springs from being themselves.

This process continues throughout the school years. If joy or playfulness bubbles up while the teacher is talking, the child invariably gets a dirty look or a reprimand. The charge is one of not paying attention. In fact, the child *was* paying attention to the inner world of his own thoughts and perceptions, but is made to feel wrong for that. If a child feels like dancing down the hallway instead of falling into line, she is considered 'disorderly' or 'uncooperative'. I can recall being reprimanded for looking out the window of my classroom when the first large snowflakes of the winter began to fall: "It's only snow, I'm sure you've seen it before!" I had been pondering the impossible fact that no two snowflakes are the same, and trying to grasp the complexity of such a universe. Snapped back to 'reality', I was being told that copying notes off a chalkboard was more important than the natural world, or my own thinking. Is that why busy adults can rush to work, barely noticing the wonder of a rising sun, or the dew on the grass? When is the last time you really looked at the sky?

Because most formal learning is based on a set curriculum, and the learning is measured by tests, such learning is rarely truly open-ended. We are not really free to think if, in the end, we must arrive at the 'right' answer. When my son was in kindergarten, parents were invited to the class at Christmas time. Each child was given the identical picture of Santa with a sack, which they were to color, inside the lines, of course. My son proceeded to pick up his pencil, instead of crayons as directed, and began to draw, on the outside of the sack, all of the toys he imagined to be inside. No fewer than three adults passed by his desk and 'helped' him out by telling him he was not doing what he was supposed to be doing.

I taught school for many years, and recall a colleague once having a child re-do a picture, because "horses are not purple." At that time, many of the materials we were directed to use with our students involved filling in the blanks with the correct answer. Teachers often used their answer key, simply looking at the blanks to see if the right word was there. If not, the question was marked wrong, generally with a big red 'X'. I would read the entire sentence, and was amazed at how often the child's 'wrong' answer was perfectly acceptable, made a lot of sense, and often indicated a deeper level of thinking than what the question demanded.

I often wondered how confusing that must have been when the child looked at his 'mistake,' realizing that his logical, well thought out interpretation was 'wrong' simply because it was not the same as the one in the answer key. Perhaps that is why many adults I meet do not trust their own thinking. They do not consider their own ideas valid, but if they read the same thing in a book, particularly if it is written by a professional, then they feel their interpretation 'must be' correct.

On the playground, children learn early that the 'popular' or more powerful children have it best. The popular girl decides who can join the game of skipping and who cannot. The best athlete decides who can join the game of soccer, and who will get to play on his team.

They learn if you make a mistake, you will be laughed at or ridiculed. If you dress differently than others, someone will have something to say about it. They see that sometimes even the teacher gangs up on the underdog, or favors the popular students. Rarely are they taught how to handle differences or conflicts with integrity. Seldom do they see that classmates are valued by adults simply for who they are, but instead, value seems to be tied to performance.

Is it any wonder children quickly tune in to the outer world, pushing their own unique inner world farther and farther into the background of their awareness? Perhaps that is why they grow into adults who are more concerned about how others see them, than with being true to their own thoughts and feelings.

'Outer-directedness' is further developed through the media. Advertisers target increasingly younger segments of the population. Children are 'programmed' to want certain toys, foods, and clothing. They identify with their 'heroes' instead of themselves. Their heroes, however, have qualities impossible for them to attain.

No girl could ever have the proportions of a Barbie because they are distortions of the human form. Nor is she likely to have the endless supply of clothes, accessories and other luxury items that just 'come with' being Barbie. Further, no girl will keep her youthful looks, perfect figure and agelessness after year, as Barbie does.

No boy could ever have the strength and agility of Superman, because his abilities are distortions as well. Few will attain the status of 'best guy in the world'. Nor will they be able to simply step into a telephone booth and transform their identity from ordinary working guy to superhero whenever the need is felt. Nonetheless, children compare themselves to these impossible figures, and from early on see how inadequate they are.

Perhaps that is why they grow up feeling 'less' than others. Maybe that is why the 'Barbie generation' spends millions sculpting and resculpting their bodies and faces, so they can look young and attractive until they die. It may also explain the billion-dollar industry that spectator sport has become. Unable to be anything even close to the superman of his youth himself, does the adult male identify with his sports hero, cheering him on to crush the opposition? Does he see the opposing team as a 'force of evil', so that he is happy to see a fight break out and the opposing team take a beating? Is this why he may get depressed when his team is knocked out of the finals: because his 'superman' failed to save the day? And is this why his self-esteem, his confidence, and his mood soar when his team wins the championship?

Not only do the media create in children a qualitative dissatisfaction, but a quantitative one as well. It is not enough to have one Barbie. Few little girls are satisfied with one Barbie once they see how many others there are, and how many their friends have. Few little boys are satisfied with one action figure, when they find that their neighbor has the whole set. Moreover, few children are satisfied with one or two sets of trading cards, because they know that whoever has the most cards has the most trading power. When interest begins to wane for one type of card, clever marketing gurus have already launched the next wave. Early on, children develop the sense of dissatisfaction for what they have, and focus much more on what they do not have.

What they do not have creates a huge void in their consciousness, and dissatisfaction eats away at them until finally the void is filled. A day or two later, the void begins to grow again. Perhaps this is why many children grow up to be adults with addictions.

How different this is from the natural world. Imagine a place where children play in the meadows and streams, chasing butterflies and watching robins teaching their young to fly: a childhood spent exploring nature's wonders. Think of a child's mind filled with the sounds of water splashing over rocks, the songs of birds, and the sound of the wind in the trees. Imagine the child who watches the newborn kittens, eyes still closed, and the way in which the mother protects and nurtures them. Think of his delight as he picks plump ripe blueberries right off the bush, tasting their natural sweetness, savoring this treat offered up by Mother Nature. Picture this child, an avid collector, his pockets filled with interesting rocks and twigs, which hold intrinsic value for him. Fascinated with the way the sunlight casts its shadows, reflecting off remaining drops of dew, this child sees things his technologically 'advanced' counterparts would never notice. Such a child, immersed in, and at one with the natural world is without ego. What remains is soul. Ego is self-consciousness. When we are one with our soul, ego *consciousness* disappears.

Unfortunately, in the Western world at least, children are born into a world filled with sights, sounds, colors and tastes that are artificial. Does a natural rainbow seem pale and disappointing compared to the vibrant ones shown in cartoons and on commercial packaging?

Further, even the youngest are exposed to images of life on television that are not real. They grow up seeing commercials showing children (just like them) looking joyful because they are playing with the advertised product. They cannot interact with those children, they cannot ask them to share that wonderful toy; they simply watch as detached outsiders, feeling that something is missing from their lives.

They begin to become conscious of themselves because of this detachment. They become conscious of sadness, disappointment, resentment, anger, and even hopelessness. In a child detached from authentic life, ego becomes strengthened at the expense of soulful awareness.

If, in addition, the child's parents or caregivers are not soulful in their interactions with the child, the detachment is compounded. Often it is the adult egos that are working to shape the child into their image of what he should be. It is ego interpretations and behaviors that are being modeled. Such a parent cannot possibly see or access the soul of the child.

Soul is accessed through soul. Sometimes the soulfulness of

the very young child triggers awareness of soul in adults. Generally, however, at an early age the child loses touch with his soul, in the same way that one loses facility in a language once known but no longer spoken. The difference here is that the child never actually spoke the language of soul, for the soul connection faded before he had the verbal fluency to express it. That is why later in life, when soul awareness can suppress itself no longer, we feel its presence, but struggle to express or define it. It feels like we are learning a new language. That is because we are.

WHAT THEN, IS SOUL?

Soul is more difficult to describe because the word has been used since long before science created the concept of ego. Just as ego is a term used to refer to certain aspects of consciousness, so soul could be viewed simply as a term referring to other aspects of consciousness. It would refer to that aspect of awareness which transcends the here and now of our lives.

If our individual egos are what differentiate us from one another, soul would be that aspect which connects us to each other and to the bigger whole of existence. Ego is a product of our minds. Soul is that non-physical part of us which existed before we could use our minds. Soul is what we feel in the presence of one in a coma, even though the individual cannot communicate with us. Soul is what draws us so powerfully to a newborn. Every mother can tell you how different each baby feels, right from the start. Soul is the very powerful presence we feel even when a loved one has passed on physically.

Because our society has not generally recognized the existence of soul, except in a religious or spiritual sense, which not all share, it has remained in the background of our collective awareness. The child is not responded to as a unique soul with its own journey. Rather, most children are considered to be more like blank slates upon which parents, teachers and society project their ideas of who he or she should be.

This may create problems right from the start, if the child is a feisty soul, but more often things tick along uneventfully. All the while the soul has been watching and waiting, patiently allowing ego to run its course, to have its day. Soul has not, however, been sitting idle.

When the time comes for soul to emerge more fully into awareness, it may begin with gentle nudges. With no response, there may be various struggles, conflicts or even crises showing up in daily life. Slowly but surely, ego begins to sense something is wrong. Ego feels a threat to its own existence, and digs in its heels.

Soul is not an antagonist. Soul does not fight with ego. Soul is a teacher. What begins to happen is that when ego is in charge, things do not go as well: pain, suffering, conflicts, and struggle often result. When ego backs off, allowing soul to peek through like the sun on a cloudy day, everything in life warms up, particularly the heart. We have access to innate wisdom beyond anything we could imagine. We may even catch a glimpse of the perfection in all things. Like the shell from which the chick emerges, ego begins to weaken, to crumble, and to fall away.

The voice of soul can now be heard. After so long it feels like a strange voice, so it is hard to trust it. It seems to invite us to let go of all that ego has so painfully and carefully built over the years. That, for many, is completely overwhelming. It is at about this time that the trouble starts.

If we had never felt the presence of soul in our lives, we might never feel sad, unfulfilled, or conflicted. We might never have the feeling that something is missing. We feel soul's presence when ego is in the background, out of the way, for it is only then that we can 'remember' the 'feel' of soul. A child in the womb is in soul-to-soul contact with its Mother. That soulful connection remains after birth, but soon physical pain or discomfort narrows the focus of awareness, bringing consciousness squarely back to the bodily sensations.

The newborn is without thought or language: this is when experience of soul is most direct. When parents first hold their child, the soul connection is so powerful that parental ego is temporarily 'blown away'. Humans are in awe of a newborn child and are often rendered temporarily speechless. Even other children are quieted by the powerful presence of the sleeping infant's soulfulness. I have often thought the story of Jesus' birth is also a metaphor for the Divine soul taking human form, which happens every time a human is born.

When we are deep in prayer, or in communion with Nature, the alignment of our soul with the Divine is so complete that there is no room for ego. These are times when we 'lose' ourselves in something infinitely more vast than our own consciousness. We feel rested, refreshed and renewed, because we have once again connected with our own souls. It is as though the gates of ego which have confined or blocked the soul energy are opened, and individual soul, like a river, mingles and joins with the ocean of the collective soul—the undercurrent of all life. There is a comfort in this blending. Such experiences form a respite for the unconscious 'homesickness' we feel, having become so detached from that which gives most comfort.

When we are deeply in love, we are touching one another's soul, and that place of shared soulfulness results in the feeling of bliss. In such moments we transcend individual egos, and connect powerfully from our souls. That is why we speak of 'soul-mates', and why such an experience leaves us feeling so free, so expansive. The walls of ego have dissolved, leaving the open fields of soul which seem endless, touching the 'forever.'

Love lasts forever on the soul level, but unfortunately, ego creates a lot of static, often drowning out the deeper levels of love.

Getting lost in art, music or anything about which we are passionate creates similar feelings of expansiveness, freedom, and bliss. It is not something outside of ourselves creating the bliss. An external event or person may trigger our own connection with soul, and *that* is bliss. Anchored in our memory is the wonderful feeling of *being soul*. It is the highest feeling a human can experience, and whether we are consciously aware of it or not, we forever yearn for it. Sometimes addictions are an unconscious attempt to return to that blissful, contented state. It is not found, however, by numbing the senses, but rather by heightening awareness naturally.

Humans throughout history have attempted to describe that ineffable aspect of being of which we may become aware only when spirit moves through it:

> ...the soul may be defined as the initial actuality of a natural *body endowed with the capacity of life.*
> *Aristotle*
> (Greek philosopher, 384-322 B.C.E.)

> *The seat of the soul is there where the inner world and the outer world meet. Where they overlap, it is in every point of overlap.*
> Novalis

> *Man is a stream whose source is hidden. Our being is descending into it from we know not whence.*

> *We live in succession, in division, in parts, in particles. Meantime within man is the soul of the whole: the wise silence: the universal beauty, to which every part and*

particle is equally related: the eternal One... We see the world piece by piece, as the sun, the moon, the animal, the tree; but the whole, of which these are the shining parts, is the soul.
    Ralph Waldo Emerson
    (American transcendentalist 1803-1882)

The soul is a breath of living spirit, that with excellent sensitivity permeates the entire body to give it life.
    Hildegard of Bingen,
    (German prophet and mystic, 1089-1179)

  The only thing we can say about soul with any certainty is that it defies any form of absolute definition. Webster's dictionary defines it as *the immaterial essence of substance, the animating principle or actuating cause of life.* This definition describes soul, but still does not say what it *is*. Like love, soul will always be described in different ways in various contexts. The word 'soul' allows us to make reference to something invisible, immeasurable, non-physical, but nonetheless 'felt' by humans since the beginning of time.

  What we might agree upon is that soul is not 'matter'; it is not of the material world. Hence, when we speak of soul, we are making a connection to the world of spirit, cosmic energy, Universal intelligence or Oneness.

  What is significant, from a scientific perspective, is that quantum physicists are beginning to *find evidence* of an underlying force or unifying principle that has been described through time, even by the most primitive people. They are finding patterns of connection, linking all that is, in one unified whole. In this there is what we can call a universal spirit, which links us all. For the purposes of our discussions here, soul is considered to be that aspect of human awareness that is in alignment with the unifying principles and patterns of the universe. It is the natural essence of each one of us, unbounded by mind, thought, ego, time or space.

THE EMERGENCE OF SOUL

As we move through life, the more distant we become from our own soul, the more unsatisfying life becomes. Despite having created all of the things ego decided we should have, we do not feel the joy. We cannot find the bliss. Perhaps we have become 'lost souls', or at the very least, we have unknowingly allowed ego to 'misguide' us.

At a subtle level, there is a feeling of living an unfulfilled life. There may be a lack of enthusiasm or happiness. The future seems to hold no promise of any significant change in our situation. It is depressing to 'have it all', yet to still feel empty, still searching. Sometimes the warning signaling alienation from soul is not so subtle.

Imagine tectonic plates of consciousness: eventually ego cannot push forward any longer without catastrophic consequences. If we are not honoring our true selves along life's journey, the wake-up call generally comes in the form of a life crisis. A relationship ends, a career flounders, there is a financial or health crisis, an adolescent runs away or addictive behaviors sabotage forward movement.

Suddenly life as we knew it seems to grind to a halt, and the full-blown life crisis triggers a crisis of identity. We not only question who we are now and who we will be, but for the first time we begin to question *who we have been* all those years. At this point, people often feel their lives are falling apart, or they, personally, are breaking down. Generally, this is felt to be a bad thing, however, if understood, the exact opposite is true.

Kazimierz Dabrowski (1964) developed a theory of 'positive

disintegration,' which considers the breakdowns we have been describing to be instrumental in the development of authentic personalities. Most people, he suggests, live their lives guided by their biological impulses (mostly self-interest) and/or by uncritical adherence to social convention.

Life crises represent the potential for personal growth as they often trigger careful personal evaluation of the world and one's values. This is a developmental process, he claims, and the answers come in listening to the heart, and resisting automatic, conditioned social answers. As we begin to discern that there are higher and lower choices (the defining moment in our personal evolution we mentioned earlier), and that we can *choose* how we interpret what we perceive, a new and powerful type of conflict emerges.

Once we see a higher choice and recognize it as an ideal, if our behavior falls short of that ideal, disharmony often follows. This may result in a drive to review and realign one's life. The individual may begin to attempt to replace lower, automatic perceptions and reactions with more consciously chosen ones. Behavior becomes less reactive, less automatic, as one consciously chooses to align behavior and responses with higher, chosen ideals.

Dabrowski also suggests that as individuals achieve higher levels of development, the level of society is raised as well. He envisioned a genuine cultivation of social interactions based on higher values. Thus, rather than viewing crisis or disintegration as negative or dysfunctional, and attempting to eliminate the symptoms, he would argue for reframing these situations so as to gain understanding and insight into life.

In other words, individuals can learn to consciously transcend biological instinct and rote socialization, and so realize the authentic humanness that lies dormant, just waiting for the light of awareness—the catalyst, which will beckon it forth.

This is the process of taming ego so the voice of soul may be heard, and may become the wisdom that guides our lives.

THE VOICES OF EGO AND SOUL

Ego speaks for itself. Ego is the self-centered child, unaware of the needs or perceptions of others. As we become more socially conscious, we learn to say the words that make it sound like we are taking others into account, but ego has its own agenda. Ego brainwashes us into believing its view of reality. Ego is right and everyone else is wrong.

The person may not always verbalize such thoughts, but they are held silently nonetheless. Imagine a young child in the sandbox who tells everyone else what part they are to play, what part of the sandbox they should use, and what they should build. This is the way ego thinks.

Soul speaks through the heart. Soul knows what is best for all. Soul is like a nurturing mother who sees the conflict, the joys and sorrows of her children, and unconditionally loves them through it. Soul is at peace, because it is unattached to the dramas of ego. Soul is the voice of wisdom, the connection with Universal intelligence. Soul is the place where we are all one: where we no longer see others as separate or different from ourselves. In that place of soul, there is no concept of ownership, right or wrong, gain or loss.

Ego is 'doing'. Soul is 'being'. Ego is 'trying'; soul is 'allowing'. Ego is polarity; soul is unity. Ego is attachment; soul is non-attachment. Ego is grounded in the world, while soul is at the same time in the world, *and* transcending it.

Ego has never left the 'town' in which it was born, while soul has travelled everywhere. Ego cannot leave, for it is of the world and has no wings to fly beyond its own limitations. Ego dies; soul is eternal. Ego is illusion. Ego is a costume that hides the true identity of the soul behind it. If we believe we are who our costume represents, then we wander aimlessly through life never understanding why we just do not feel like ourselves. We forever have the sense that something is missing. We search for the knowledge, the experiences, the partner, the material possessions, the geographical location, or the spiritual path that might make us feel at peace. However, it is ego that is doing the searching, and continues to search externally.

Peace is not to be found there, and in its constant searching, ego only makes things worse. However, even the most enlightened CEO would have a difficult time cutting his own position, even if it is what is best for the company. Ego holds on, even as its position becomes increasingly obsolete.

WHEN EGO DIRECTS LIFE

Ego is in a constant state of contradiction. Ego tries to win, to be right, to gain control, to overcome, to be better. The problem is that when ego wins, the person loses. When there is no thought of winning, being right, gaining control, overcoming or being better than, ego has lost, but the person wins. When ego can remain respectfully in the background, the whole win/lose dichotomy is transcended.

The person feels fulfilled, at peace and contented, even though things are not perfect. Or rather, the person sees the perfection in the way things are. Soul knows that things unfold as they should. Ego wants things to unfold according to its wishes. In fighting against what is natural to soul, ego creates untold pain for itself. Those pains are the struggles of life. What, specifically, are they?

If we want to find where ego is actively sabotaging the soul's higher wisdom, we can look at those areas where humans ex-

perience conflict or dis-ease. They include, but are not limited to the following:
- conflict with youngsters, adolescents or grown children
- conflict with parents
- relationship struggles
- self-esteem issues
- addictions
- anger issues
- workplace issues
- eating disorders
- depression
- anxiety
- difficulty managing finances
- blocked creativity
- communication problems
- suicide
- compromised physical and emotional health

Few individuals go through life untouched by at least some of the above difficulties. Each is a context providing an opportunity to engage the soul's wisdom. Because so few know how to really access that wisdom, ego uses the same strategies again and again. Things become worse instead of better. Sometimes the same struggles repeat themselves over and over, with different people or situations each time.

Life becomes characterized by emotional pain, competition (win-lose), dissonance, polarity, conditional love and acceptance, and imbalance. It is easy to be knocked off center. It feels like 'here we go again', as we wonder why the same things keep happening, or why we seem to attract the same kinds of people or situations into our lives, bringing us the same kind of grief we have experienced before.

This is an illusion. What is really happening is that we are *being* the same kind of person, led by the same ego, (even if it disguises itself) doing the same things, creating the same problems. We will continue doing this until we learn to listen to the voice of soul.

SOUL DIRECTED LIFE

What happens when ego is tamed, and soul's wisdom is operational in our lives? Life does not suddenly become free of problems, but fewer of them are of our own making. People will die, jobs will be lost, finances may be difficult, children will try us, relationships will end, but we will perceive the events of life in a different light. Consequently responses will be different.

Instead of fighting against the tides of life, we begin to flow with them. We see the bigger picture, and come to understand how our responses will determine whether outcomes will be painful or peaceful, whether we will regress to a more primitive state, or use the situation as a springboard for growth. When life is interpreted from the perspective of understanding, compassion and acceptance, as opposed to judgement and blame, we are then able to create the following:
- mutually respectful relationships between parents and children
- couples' relationships based on trust, respect, integrity and mutual growth
- productive, satisfying communication
- effective skills for problem resolution
- self-validation
- balanced mood
- relaxed approach to life
- increased creativity as an expression of individuality
- release of addictions and addictive behaviors

- elimination of anger reactions
- mature, functional responses to workplace issues
- financial responsibility, and respect for money as a form of energy
- higher levels of physical and emotional health

Our lives become characterized by peace, harmony, loving connections, contentment, balance, reverence, and serenity. We could say that we are creating happiness, but it is a state that is qualitatively different from the happiness we feel when ego needs are satisfied. The happiness that comes from winning, getting the highest score, receiving a compliment, or getting a raise is short lived. Soon there will be another competition, another arena where ego tests itself. The happiness of ego is a roller-coaster ride.

The happiness of soulful living is like peacefully rowing across still water on a beautiful, endless day. Clouds may come and temporarily block the sun, or waves may come up, but still, you row peacefully, because the water carries you and the quality of the journey is more important than the destination.

Does this mean there will never be another crisis? Unfortunately not. What *will* be different is your perception of what we used to call crises. Unfortunate events may occur, but understanding the human journey from a broader perspective allows for greater levels of acceptance. You will come to see which difficulties are a result of ego qualities sneaking in to thoughts and actions, and which, though not self-created, nonetheless are challenges to your ability to transcend the demands or preferences of ego.

As we release our attachment to ego and its perceptions of how life 'should' be, we develop the qualities of harmony, balance, and serenity. Others are drawn to us because of that strong, peaceful energy, and take comfort in our wisdom. *Life* does not become serene, harmonized and balanced. *We* do.

THE LINK TO SPIRITUALITY

Generally, the qualities we have here been attributing to soul consciousness have tended to be associated with more spiritual endeavors. Whether we are talking about the traditional golden rule: "do unto others as you would have them do unto you", the karmic principle of "what goes around comes around", or the more esoteric traditions of the world's many religions, there often has been a separation between the 'spiritual' and practical. Always, there have been those who work diligently to incorporate the highest principles of their spiritual beliefs into all facets of daily life, but more commonly, when it comes to the nitty-gritty of survival in the playground, the village, or the boardroom, the ego takes over. Spirit has its place: in the temple, the church, or the synagogue; but out in the world it has still been survival of the fittest, the strongest, or the most powerful.

As we continue to evolve in consciousness, we grow to realize such a separation does not work. Only those who remain unconscious can pray for the blessings of a supreme power one day, inflict harm, injustice, or behave irreverently towards any living thing the next, and not feel any inner conflict.

As we come to understand the holographic nature of our inner and outer universes, we realize that always, every thought or action, no matter how small, is reflected in the spectrum of our life experiences. Each contributes to the definition of who we are, and constitutes an aspect of the world we are creating for ourselves. Each also impacts the outer world.

All communication, through word or deed, is energy. What then, is the link to spirituality? We are all part of an energy system: the same energy system that created and maintains the stars in the heavens, the planets in their orbits, the changing of the seasons, and the songs of the birds. This cosmic energy is movement, but more than that, it is *intelligent* movement. This energy contains information, which directs the movement of atoms, molecules, cellular processes, and the development of a fetus.

Everything in the universe is vibrating. The thirteenth century poet, Rumi, wrote of 'atoms dancing.' Modern scientists have found that, indeed, nothing is really solid. Instead, atoms, dancing to an unseen beat, exist in a connecting space—space between atoms, space between stars. It is through this medium of space that any living, vibrating thing, be it a star or a thought, sends its message to the whole universe.

This energy, underlying, permeating, surrounding everything that is, has been described throughout history and in various cultures: *Prana* in Sanskrit, *Chi* in Chinese, *Mana* in Polynesian. Findings from the modern scientific field of quantum physics show that, in the quantum world of which our body's cells are a part, there are no barriers.

Mass, energy and information are one, time is relative, and separateness of any kind is an illusion. According to this principle of nonlocality, we all participate in, and contribute to a subtle energy field—a timeless connection. Nonlocality refers to that energetic intelligence field. All that is, has been or ever will be is a part of this field.

Spirituality is the human experience of this transcendental reality beyond the limits of personality. Spiritual awakening has been a natural human experience throughout the ages, and, no doubt, the birthplace of all religions. Spirit is the name we have given to that force, that energy which vibrates within us and beyond us, and connects us all, to each other and all that is.

Spirit, or Universal energy, manifests in humans as life force. Humans are energy systems, designed to receive and transmit this energy. When mediated by soul it flows, via the heart, freely through the individual in a harmonious, balanced way. When mediated by ego, it passes through the filter of mind, and becomes constricted, re-directed, controlled, blocked, or distorted.

Human emotions are the feedback system, or control panel, indicating how the body-mind is processing the life force energy. Soulful, heart-based movement of energy creates balanced states, feelings of understanding, acceptance, and compassion. Ego-based, mind-mediated movement of energy creates duality, polarity, competition, judgment, and other forms of fragmentation of the life force energy. This creates feelings of pain, stress, hopelessness, anxiety, restlessness, and dissatisfaction.

When communication is based on ego interpretation, the energy circulates within a closed system, from ego to ego and back again. Often the same energy keeps cycling through the system, and ego creates resistance or blockages. When communication is based on soul interpretation, the energy is more open. It seems to come from somewhere outside of ourselves, like a fresh breeze blowing off the ocean. It flows *through us* as opposed to originating *within* us. It moves through an open system.

When we open our hearts, an open-ended pathway unfolds whereby compassion or understanding flows through us and out into the world. It is an energy seeming always new, fresh, and in abundant supply.

Everyone has access to this spiritual energy. Some access it when they pray, thus associating it with the church, synagogue, temple or other place of worship, and the higher power there recognized. Some find it when they are out in the natural world, surrounded by the magnificence and diversity of our planet, thereby associating it with nature. Others access it through meditative techniques, and understand it in terms of transcending the here and now. They associate this spiritual energy with enlightenment, moving into a state of oneness, or accessing their 'higher self'.

When witnessing a birth, or being present at the moment of another's death, we are often swept up by the powerful energy of spirit that is present. Sometimes these events in themselves connect one squarely with their own spiritual energy, and can be powerfully transformative.

All of the above are valid spiritual experiences mediated by something outside of ourselves, or specific techniques. They are spiritual pathways. We are at a place now, where in addition to these pathways, we are learning to access that spiritual energy independent of beliefs, techniques or situations in our lives.

We *are* spiritual beings. We have done many things to *access* that aspect of our being. We are finding now, as we understand the functioning of ego, and learn to *choose* a different perspective, we can allow ego to step out of the way. When we do this, we are no longer accessing spirit: we are *being* spirit. With ego in the background, we experience soul. The energy of soul is spiritual energy.

What is most profound about emerging human consciousness is the recognition that viewing spirituality as a separate aspect of humanness has been an illusion. Spirituality is not separate from physicality, emotionality, or reality.

It is ego-mind that has created the separation. It has done this in the same way humans created the idea the Earth was flat. Why did they think that? Because they simply could not see the bigger picture of which they were a part. The nature of the evolution of knowledge has been a putting together of the little parts, until a larger pattern begins to emerge.

We stand now at the dawning of a new era in understanding. Surprisingly, it is not the philosophers or the spiritual leaders who are leading us to see the interconnectedness of things spiritual and things physical, and the importance of expanding our perceptions about those connections. It is the modern day scientists.

They are showing how individual values and behaviors contribute to, or detract from our evolutionary progression as a species; they are demonstrating the connection between our interpretations and responses to the world and our *physical survival.* You will see that the choice discussed earlier, between ego interpretations and soul interpretations, affects not only the quality of life, but the *quantity* as well.

Ego interpretations lead to certain emotions that create toxic effects at the cellular level that can *shorten* our lives. Thus, learning to choose how we are going to interpret what we perceive not only assists us in moving to the next stage in the evolutionary progression, but also may be critical to our physical survival.

Whether this process is a spiritual endeavor becomes a moot point. The critical point affecting all of us, regardless of our spiritual orientation or belief systems, is that developing the ability to choose consciously is essential for both individual and species survival.

Not knowing that we *could* choose has resulted in patterns within individuals, communities, and countries, and have been ego-dominated. Such patterns result in greater isolation, individualism, and selfishness. In individuals this manifests as stress related to relationships, children, finances, work situations, and even freeway driving. At the level of communities and countries it manifests as divisiveness, competition, lack of integrity in government or in elected officials, conflict, and even war.

The first step in changing the old patterns is awareness of the ability to make conscious choices. Equally important is understanding the consequences of *not* learning to do so. With such interdependence between body, mind, and soul, all three must move forward together.

The next chapter will show in greater detail how science has found links between mind, body, and perhaps even the soul. You will see how the decision to interpret and respond to life from an ego-based perspective can compromise physical health, possibly contributing to premature death. You will also see growing evidence supporting the premise that moving towards the soul-based end of the awareness continuum is strongly associated with a strengthened immune system, higher levels of physical and emotional health, and therefore an increased life span.

Chapter 2

SCIENCE CONNECTS BODY, MIND AND SOUL

Psychoneuroimmunology is a relatively new scientific discipline, which studies how the mind influences the body's well-being. It delves into the realm of how neurological pathways link the immune system and the brain. Researchers are finding convincing evidence that thoughts, moods, emotions and belief systems have a fundamental impact on some of the body's basic health and healing mechanisms.

EMOTIONS AND THE IMMUNE SYSTEM

Dr. Candace Pert, research professor in the department of physiology and biophysics at Georgetown University Medical Center in Washington, D.C., and author of *The Molecules of Emotion: Why We Feel the Way We Feel*, suggests that cells communicate with each other via emotions, as carried by peptide biochemicals, to keep us operating as an integrated whole. She believes that humans are designed, from an evolutionary perspective, to achieve intimate, loving relationships, and that negative emotions such as alienation, hostility, depression, cynicism and isolation are so toxic because they are not natural states.

How can the above qualities affect our physical health? Psychoneuroimmunology has shown an intimate relationship between cells of the immune system and cells of the nervous system. This relationship is mediated by chemical messengers called cytokinins, which are secreted into the bloodstream (immune system) or the cerebro-spinal fluid (nervous system). Cytokinins work in either stimulatory or inhibitory ways on the cell surface receptors of immune and nerve cells. They are significant, since only 2% of neuronal communication is electrical and across a synapse, the remaining 98% is chemical.

This chemical communication is mediated by small chains of amino-acids called peptides, and cytokinins are a special class of those peptides. Dr. Candace Pert called these peptides the "molecules of emotion". Our mental-emotional state determines our level of health by determining which peptides and cytokinins are produced.

Depression has been found to be the single most detrimental factor in suppression of the immune system: it causes the nervous system to produce inhibitory cytokinins. The second most detrimental factor has been found to be chronic stress. Chronic stress causes the nervous system to produce stimulatory cytokinins resulting in overstimulation of the immune system and 'burn-out'.

If we are not living in alignment with our highest evolutionary potential, imbalanced on the side of ego-based reactions rather than soul-based perceptions, then negative situations and emotions are often created. Let's look, in a little more detail, at the way in which negative situations and emotions compromise health.

Other scientists support the findings of Dr. Pert, that the brain and nervous system are closely connected to the immune system, as is the endocrine system. The body and mind comprise an interconnected system, the functioning of the parts of which cannot be understood in isolation. Henry Dreher, in *The Immune Power Personality*, says the nervous, endocrine and immune systems 'talk' to each other in a language made up of 'cell products'. He describes a 'superhighway of cellular information.' Brain chemicals called neurotransmitters mediate our thoughts and feelings. However, these chemicals are not limited to the brain, but circulate throughout our whole system, functioning as carriers of our emotions. *Herein lies the direct connection between our perception of the world, our emotional reactions, our immune system and our physical health.*

Negative or distressing thoughts, attitudes or reactions directly impact the immune system. Interestingly, optimum health, even in terms of immune functioning, is a result of balance. Certain autoimmune diseases are a result of overactivity of the immune system, creating as many problems as an underactive or weakened immune system.

What has been clearly demonstrated, scientifically, over the past decades is the harmful effect upon health of certain personality traits, such as negativity, hostility, and distrust. Science is still in the early stages of understanding the traits and behaviors that contribute to health, but the implications are becoming increasingly clear.

STRESS AND DISTRESS

Feelings of helplessness, hopelessness, and alienation have been shown to negatively affect the immune system, specifically by a reduction in the activity of those immune cells, which ward off disease. Stress has been associated with compromised health, but Dreher makes the significant point that it is not stress in itself, but rather *how we cope with stress*, that is significant. He argues that our psychological resources are far more important than our stressors. I would add to that the impact of spiritual resources, in the broadest sense.

Dreher differentiates between 'stress' and 'distress.' He says that stress is the objective event: whatever it is that is happening. Distress is the inner reaction. Distress results in feelings of hopelessness, helplessness, anxiety, depression, isolation, panic, repressed or expressed rage, and/or fatigue. Distress signals that what we are doing is not working.

Often the treatment of these symptoms falls into the category of what has been called first order change—that is, change occurring within a system which itself remains unchanged. We may reduce anxiety through relaxation training, or alleviate depression with medication, but we are treating *symptoms* rather than changing *the system which produces them.* If distress is the inner reaction, then second order change (altering the system itself) would mean changing *the unconscious pattern of interpretation, action and reaction which has produced the distressed state in the first place.* It would mean transcending the realm of ego perceptions, which invariably invite reactions. Later chapters will address this process. It is significant to mention it here so that you can see how the premise of this book is connected to what we are learning from modern medical scientists, but then takes the process one 'leap' further. It is that leap which will allow for 'real' change.

Dreher sees the desired goals of an integrated mindbody system as balance and harmony, communication and connectedness. Reaching these goals creates "a state of grace, one in which body and spirit are united, one in which our ability to heal and repair ourselves is potentially boundless." Real-

Science Connects Body and Soul

izing our authentic selves, he says, is a very powerful health prescription.

HEALING

Dean Ornish, M.D., in his book, *Love and Survival – The Scientific Basis for the Healing Power of Intimacy*, reports hundreds of documented scientific studies showing that:
> *...anything that promotes feelings of love and intimacy is healing; anything that promotes isolation, separation, loneliness, loss, hostility, anger, cynicism, depression, alienation, and related feelings often leads to suffering, disease, and premature death from all causes.*

Conversely, and perhaps astoundingly, Ornish and his colleagues found the reverse also to be true. They found the progress of even coronary heart disease could be reversed. Factors in such reversals included discovering sources of peace, joy and wellbeing, learning to communicate more intimately with loved ones, creating a healthy community of family and friends, developing increased empathy and compassion for self and others, and experiencing the transcendent interconnectedness of all life. These qualities are all associated with a soulful interpretation and approach to life. In fact, we can see how ego-based interpretations and reactions would render attainment of those qualities virtually impossible, but furthermore, would contribute to diseased states. Ornish contends the real epidemic in our culture is not only physical heart disease, but what he calls *emotional and spiritual heart disease*, characterized by feelings of isolation, alienation and depression.

Dr. Paul Pearsall, psychoneuroimmunologist and author of *The Heart's Code: Tapping the Wisdom and Power of Our Heart*

Energy, takes the discussion one step further, introducing the concept of soul into the psychoneuroimmunological loop. He argues that the heart is the conveyor of a code representing the soul. He suggests we have a deep inner wisdom that will guide us along a healthy evolutionary pathway, and the way we can access it is through the heart. He suggests science may have finally contacted the human soul:

Science has recently discovered three startling new possibilities regarding how we think, feel, love, heal and find meaning in our life. This research suggests that the heart thinks, cells remember, and that both of these processes are related to an as yet mysterious, extremely powerful, but very subtle energy with properties unlike any other known force. If the preliminary insights regarding these prospects continue to be verified, science may be taking the first tentative steps to understanding the energy of the human spirit and the coded information that is the human soul.

Pearsall argues that the heart is the major energy center of the body, and conveyor of the soul's code. He uses the term 'energy cardiology' as he explains that, in it's own way, the heart perceives and reacts to the outside world. It communicates what he calls an 'info-energetic code' of that reaction through the circulatory system, which, with its network of vessels and cells, becomes an energy and information network. He suggests soul may be, in part, a kind of cellular, info-energetic program. The heart, he believes, is so much more than a pump! In fact, he sees it as having a mind of its own, and being the vital link between mind and body.

Pearsall reminds us that while Plato and Hippocrates saw the brain as the central aspect of the human essence, and to Aristotle it was the heart that was the seat of the soul, all three agreed that life depends on the subtle energy of the heart. Pearsall, with the advantage of findings of modern science, links mind, brain, heart and the 'subtle energy': he suggests that *the heart joins with the brain and the body to form the physical manifestation of the soul.*

SOUL AND HEALING

This is a powerful suggestion about how all of the parts of the body-mind function within the closed system that is a human being. Increasingly though, we are realizing the human is *not* a closed system at all! It is more accurate to see humans as one *cell* within the larger organism in which it is situated. That larger organism is nothing less than the entire Universe.

In such a model, what then is this energy we are calling *soul:* what is it that is being physically manifested within us? Deepak Chopra, M.D., whose teaching bridges modern science and Eastern spirituality, might call it the Conscious Energy Field. Other spiritual teachers might call it God Consciousness. Karl Pribram, physicist, might call it our experience of the holographic field. Brian Swimme, cosmologist, might describe it as our individual experience of the energetic unfolding of matter, mind, intelligence and life, that began with the primeval fireball. He might say it is the awakening of the Cosmos *through* human consciousness: the only way the Cosmos *can* be aware of itself. Swimme says there is no such thing as a disconnected thing: "each thing emerged from the primeval fireball, and nothing can remove the primordial link this establishes with every other thing in the Universe, no matter how distant." Perhaps soul then, is the energy or awareness we feel when we *allow* ourselves to consciously *feel* that connection with the boundless, timeless, whole.

We cannot *think* it. Thinking is abstract, conceptual, and

limited. Animals and plants, rocks and oceans share that connectedness with the whole without any ability to *think* about it. A brain is not a prerequisite for soul. Primitive humans *recognized* soul in all things. It has been argued that in the later stages of human evolution, particularly in Western civilization, the emphasis on the logical, analytical, language-based thinking of the left brain hemisphere has resulted in a detachment from heart-knowing and soul connection.

Our connection to heart/soul knowing is further compromised by the fact that the more rational higher brain is often overridden by the hypersensitive lower brain, thereby reducing any emotional intelligence the brain could derive from the heart. Dr. Pearsall describes the brain as more "protectively reptilian, paleomammalian and immaturely emotional than it is reflective, considerate and patient." Rational thinking is not primary when it comes to the brain's reactive survival instincts, he argues, and "enhancing the self takes precedence over regard for the welfare of others." The brain is functional: its goal is to keep us alive, orchestrating a pleasurable life.

Connection, loving and caring, Pearsall says, are not the territory of the brain, but seep in as expressions of the heart's code. Where Dreher saw distress as a result of ineffective coping, Pearsall relates it to heartlessness: a heartless world of alienation, disconnection, depression, failed or abusive relationships, violence and a speeded-up life which leaves no time for reflection, connection, balance or joy. We might also say that heartlessness blocks our awareness of that primordial link and thus our connection to the larger whole, so that soul cannot manifest within our being. Is it any wonder that in characterizing people suffering from the above qualities, we use the term 'lost soul'? The soul, however, is not lost, but lays dormant, waiting to be set free.

THE ROLE OF SOUL IN HUMAN EVOLUTION

Soul is the energy of the Universe manifesting within us. A body is just a body, with the same basic three-dimensional parts and functions as other bodies. The energy of the Universe, refracted through the prism of individual consciousness, results in an experience of soul that is both common to all, and unique to each.

When we tune in to our souls, we paradoxically and simultaneously experience oneness and uniqueness. We transcend polarity, space and time. Energy moves and circulates. Nothing is static. We are both receivers and transmitters of that energy.

In physical terms, the human mind/body is an energy system. Information is carried through structures such as molecules, genes, and DNA cells, all of which miraculously remember and communicate in order to support not only the operation of the human system, but continuation of the human species.

As Dr. Candace Pert suggests, emotions, carried by peptide biochemicals, are the medium by which cells communicate to maintain a balanced, natural state. Science continues to provide evidence that emotional reactions directly affect health. Stress, for example, stimulates the perpetual release of the hormones adrenaline, noradrenaline and cortisol into the bloodstream. Excess levels of these hormones cause the immune system to shut down.

Stress, along with hostility, anger, and depression can lead to illness and even death. Negative emotions, as Dr. Pert has shown, are toxic to a balanced, natural state. At its core, the natural human state is directed towards wholeness and integration, which is characterized by loving relationships and positive emotions. This state is correlated with a strengthened immune system, and more efficient physical functioning, particularly for the cardiovascular system. This means, simply, better health. Consequently, the natural state is pro-evolutionary.

Life will always present us with challenges, however, it is not the challenges themselves that affect health, but rather the way we react to those challenges. Actually, it is our *perception* of the events, not the events themselves, which is significant.

We can learn to *choose* perceptions that are healthful and productive. When mental and emotional reactions to life produce frustration, anxiety or indecision, potentially toxic stress hormones are released into the body/mind system. This not only drains energy, but also distorts perspectives. *Managing* stress or *controlling* reactions may settle things down some, but neither changes the underlying *perceptions* of the person nor the situation that is triggering the reactions. This is a key point.

The reactions resulting from ego perceptions will continue to create difficulties, block intelligent choices, and create outcomes that maintain struggles in life. All processes in the natural world tend towards balance, and this is true of the human body/mind. In fact, the human heart responds to imbalance in a predictable, measurable way.

Heart-rate variability (HRV) is a measure of how the heart rate speeds up and slows down, and the patterns of these changes. These changes are influenced by any input, either from the brain, such as thoughts, or stimulation from the environment. They are markedly influenced by emotions.

The heart and brain communicate via signals between the two, and thus regulate heart-rate and blood pressure. It is the interaction between these two signals that creates variation in the heartbeat. Heart-rate variability indicates the balance between the sympathetic and parasympathetic nervous systems. The sympathetic system increases heart-rate and the secretion of adrenal hormones, while the parasympathetic system slows heart-rate and has a relaxing, protective role. Good health is dependent upon proper function and balance between the two.

Frustration and anger result in a heart-rate variability pattern that is random and jerky, while sincere, positive feeling states can produce very ordered, coherent patterns. What do these patterns indicate about what is occurring in the body? Emotions such as anger, frustration, and impatience put the nervous system out of balance. Blood vessels constrict, blood pressure rises, and energy is wasted. Over time, if these emotions occur consistently, hypertension and an increased risk of heart disease result.

On the other hand, positive feeling states create heart-rate variability patterns that reflect cardiovascular efficiency. The sympathetic and parasympathetic nervous systems are working together, rather than fighting each other. They are 'in sync'. The scientific term for this is *entrainment,* which implies a high degree of synchronization, efficiency and coherent communication. In practical terms, it means the head, heart, thoughts and feelings are aligned, working harmoniously together, resulting in clarity and balance. Naturally, you feel better.

As Dr. Pearsall has suggested, the heart functions with its own 'brain', or complex nervous system. Its nerve cells or centers send messages via neurotransmitters and proteins. The heart also can learn and remember. Heart-centered thoughts and behaviors can profoundly impact the brain and its functions, affecting perception, emotion and learning abilities.

Scientists can also utilize electrocardiograms to see what is happening to electrical patterns in the heart when we experience emotions. They have found that emotions such as hostility, depression, frustration, worry and anxiety result in what they call an incoherent spectrum, meaning the frequencies are scattered and disordered.

Emotions such as love, caring, compassion and appreciation produce a coherent spectrum, because the electrical energy is ordered and harmonious. Significantly, this energy, be it disordered or harmonious, is continuously radiated to every cell in the body.

Not only do positive emotions bring measurable changes to the heart-rate patterns and electrical activity in the body, but they can also enhance the immune system. We have discussed how episodes of anger and frustration can create hormonal imbalances, which can compromise immune system functioning. High levels of the 'stress hormone', cortisol, can even damage brain cells. Another hormone, DHEA, is often called the 'anti-aging' hormone because of its beneficial effects. Research has shown that inducing positive emotional states in subjects not only reduces the cortisol levels, but also increases levels of DHEA.

Even immune system antibodies are affected by emotions. IgA is one such antibody, which defends the body against colds, flu and respiratory or urinary tract infections. Researchers have found that even *remembering* an upsetting episode and recalling the emotions felt can result in a decrease in IgA, which can last several hours. Conversely, focusing on genuine caring feelings has been shown to increase the levels of this antibody.

Clearly, maintaining consistency in positive thoughts, attitudes, and behaviors improves and maintains physical health, thus improving the quality of life for an individual. Other than prolonging the lives of individuals, can the choice of perceptions and the consequent emotions have a more general pro-evolutionary effect? We already know that mediation and arbitration are more pro-evolutionary than an eye-for-an-eye; but, do the subtleties implied by these scientific measurements regarding the impact of emotion on human energy and chemistry, have deeper implications?

Interestingly, the answer to that question is affirmative. Some researchers are suggesting the electrical waves produced in our hearts are not only transmitted to every cell of the body, but, like radio waves, are transmitted *outside* of the body as well. Our brains can pick up information from the energy field radiated by the hearts of others. This is why you can feel the energy in a room, or the reason others may be uncomfortable around a couple in conflict, even if they are trying to hide it.

What this means is that our inner disordered state can affect others in our environment negatively; and, conversely, a coherent, balanced inner state can radiate harmonious energy outwards. Our perceptions and emotions affect the neural circuitry of the brain. Whether we are 'learning' healthy responses, or stressful reactions, we are hardwiring that pattern into our system. We ourselves can be toxic to the environment! We can also be healing. We can contribute to perpetuating patterns, which support healthy evolution, or unhealthy decline.

A further pro-evolutionary finding is that those who have a social motivation to establish supportive, caring relationships with others, and who emanate warm, loving energy, have decreased levels of stress hormones and higher levels of IgA, *even during times of stress*. Being kind, loving, understanding, accepting and compassionate towards others and ourselves, enhances the well-being and longevity of both individual and species. It would seem that the body has been designed to function best when aligned with soul-based qualities.

If soul is the energy of the universe manifesting in physical form, then allowing the energy to flow freely through us is healthy, and allowing ego to block that free flow is as damaging to the body as putting dirty fuel in a vehicle. The vehicle does not go as well, but also can be permanently damaged.

The universe, and everything in it, is evolving through a process of energy transformation. Moving, flowing energy is growth, expansion and evolution. Blocked energy is stagnation, contraction and death. Blocked energy is to the human soul what blocked arteries are to the human body. When soul energy flows through us, we radiate joy, love, enthusiasm, creativity, serenity and oneness with nature. When soul energy is blocked by the constraints of ego consciousness, we project struggle, pain, imbalance and conflict.

Evolution is increasingly supported as we move farther away from ego consciousness, towards the natural state of soul consciousness. Once we have awareness of these levels, we can *choose* to function in more soulful ways.

As we journey through life, we may at times be quite soulful, and at other times find ourselves stuck back in ego reactions. The process of human evolution leads naturally, however, in the direction of soulfulness.

We can see, within human civilization, there are impulses that lead to unhealthy evolution of our species and destruction of our planet, and those that support the healthy evolution of both species and planet. We are at a turning point, because we have reached the stage in our evolution where, as never before, we understand the implications of our actions at every level from the cellular to the planetary.

We also are recognizing our ability to make conscious choices, which, at the most intimate level, can alter our biochemistry, and at the most expansive level, can affect the ecosystem. We can, for the first time in human history, consciously participate in the co-creation of the future of our species and our planet.

Nature, in her genius, has built in to each one of us a powerful compass to lead us in the direction of individual, species, planetary, and universal wholeness. The compass is the heart. It leads us directly to soul.

HEART AND SOUL

It would seem that ego speaks more through the brain, while soul whispers its message to the heart. Pearsall refers to self-help strategies which keep us in a perpetual state of recovery (first order change), suggesting that considering new ways of understanding our own responsibilities, limitations and emotional impacts on others (second order change), is more important than learning new techniques of self-actualization.

He says the heart knows success cannot be *pursued,* but must *ensue* "as a result of a more gentle, balanced, caring, connected and loving orientation to the world." Things happen in life that are beyond our control, and from them, we can learn to "stop trying and start being."

While both heart and brain influence the entire body, Pearsall notes the heart alone, as it beats rhythmically, "provides a constantly resonating reminder that we are sending and receiving the information of our soul." This info-energy is stored at every level of cellular structure.

Moreover, the suggestion is that what has happened to any and all of us is forever stored within the cells and molecules of each of us. All cells share common cellular memories, and because memories are a form of energy, they can never be destroyed. What the cells remember, Pearsall says, "is the code of the eternal collective soul as represented in this energy we share with everyone and everything."

How do we tap into, or recognize this code of the eternal collective soul? Pearsall describes a process he calls 'cardio-contemplation'—a state that allows one to extract information about the soul via the heart energy. He says it seems to be a way of 'being' more than a way of 'doing'. Essentially it means tuning in to the heart energy. The process is likened to meditation, but with a unique focus on the heart. Tapping into this heart energy allows us to contact our soul, or at any rate, to be more soulful. As we discussed in Chapter one, soul is a word that is used in many different ways. Historically, great thinkers from Keats to Michelangelo have made reference to a subtle energetic power that is an animating force of the human spirit; it expresses our own soul, and connects us to all other souls.

Now modern scientists, the quantum physicists, base their theories of the cosmos on an infinitely pervasive energetic intelligence, invisible to mechanical instruments.

The principle of nonlocality describes a quantum world—including the cells of our own bodies—in which mass, energy and information are all one, where there are no barriers, and where time is relative. There is an info-energetic memory, which connects everything, and separateness is an illusion of the mind.

That energetic intelligence belongs to what we call the higher power, that to which in our own tradition we might pray. It is a cosmic intelligence, an ocean out of which the atoms continually constitute and reconstitute to form all that we see as reality. Spirituality is the process of connecting with that pervasive intelligence, and soul is the aspect of consciousness that makes the connection.

The connecting point for this, according to Pearsall, is the heart. Connecting heart to heart, being soulful, he says, "requires invitation instead of demand, being receptive instead of prejudicial in our expectations, and being accepting and welcoming instead of seductive and controlling."

The aspect of humans that is demanding, prejudicial in expectations, seductive, and controlling is the ego, and is based on the workings of the brain. The part that is inviting, receptive, accepting, and welcoming is the soul, accessed and expressed through the heart. Science is proving, without a doubt, that those qualities associated with ego compromise health. More remarkably, it is beginning to show, as described earlier, that those qualities associated with soul not only contribute to health, but also can strengthen the immune system, and even *reverse* illness.

IMPLICATIONS

Clearly, compelling scientific evidence continues to reveal that the old ways of reacting to life are not healthy. In recent decades we have taken great leaps in our understanding of what constitutes a healthy diet and a healthy body. In the coming decades, we will see similar shifts in what we can call the 'ecology of consciousness'. In the same way that physical health is powerfully affected by whether we have an ego-based or soul-based orientation, so the quality of our emotional lives, our relationships, how we raise our children, and how we define and achieve career success, are also dramatically dependent upon the orientation we choose.

Change begins with first steps. The first step in this next major evolutionary shift is to understand the continuum of consciousness, which moves from an ego-based to a soul-based perspective, and to locate where *we* are on that continuum. Then, we must learn to recognize choice points when they arise, and to choose a path of evolved consciousness. Our physical, emotional, spiritual, and even global health depends upon it.

The purpose of this book is to accelerate your awareness and understanding of this evolutionary process, and to provide tools to create the inner peace and happiness that your soul desires for you, so that you may consciously co-create the life you were meant to live.

In order to do this, it is important to be aware of, and to more fully understand, the continuum of consciousness to which I have been referring. We cannot really chart a path, moving away from ego consciousness and towards soul consciousness without first having a map of the territory. The next chapter will provide just that.

Chapter 3

THE CONTINUUM OF AWARENESS AND BEHAVOR

EGO 'THINKING AND SOUL 'KNOWING'

How do we live soulfully? Is there a way to transcend the struggles, the emotional quicksand into which untamed ego so effectively draws us? The answer is yes, but first we must understand the patterns associated with 'ego thinking', and those associated with 'soul knowing'. It is the thinking patterns that create the behaviors, the ensuing outcomes, and even the themes in our lives.

Recall earlier we said ego, made up of impulses and drives towards self-satisfaction, sees everything in relation to itself. It judges the experiences of life as 'good' or 'bad', 'favorable' or 'unfavorable', 'positive' or 'negative', based on the extent to which those experiences further, or frustrate, ego's agenda. Neutral experiences are virtually ignored, having little positive or negative value.

The situations ego judges as 'good' are those where it senses something is to be gained; consequently, there may be a sense of accomplishment, reward, satisfaction, pride, personal gain, and increased self-esteem. The situations judged as 'bad' are those where there is a sense of loss, sorrow, dissatisfaction, lowered self-esteem and loss of control. Ego must remain constantly vigilant, like a king guarding his kingdom, making sure that nothing is being lost.

When 'good' things happen, ego is on a high. When 'bad' things happen, ego goes into a place of polarity (good-guy, bad-guy), becomes adversarial and resentful, confrontational or punishing. These qualities are either acted out, creating stress and conflict, or held in, causing the individual to experience depression, anxiety, headaches, stomach aches, tense muscles, over or under-eating, substance abuse, or other physical or emotional symptoms.

Ego interpretations are also associated with co-dependence. Co-dependence means our source of happiness or fulfillment is outside ourselves: one's mood or sense of well-being is directly related to the behaviors of others, or the events in our lives. Like a kite flying in the wind, the co-dependent person depends on an outside force to stay afloat. If that force is not there, ego comes crashing down.

Throughout this book you will see examples of situations in which ego creates negative outcomes. Without awareness or consciousness about one's own processes, these outcomes become part of a vicious cycle. Such a cycle creates a life of stress and struggle, pain and conflict, which in turn compromises emotional and physical health.

Soul-knowing comes from a completely different place, and results in quite different outcomes. Soul, like a referee in a hockey game, knows what is right regardless of the passions flaring in ego.

Soul does not take sides, for soul-knowing comes from a level far beyond polarity and the drama of the situation. A three-year old may not be easily enticed to throw the ball to Daddy, for fear of losing the ball. A six-year old understands the game, and releases the ball easily. Soul, like the older child in the example, does not hold on to things for then the process would stop.

What is the process that would stop? It is the journey to wholeness, to the fulfillment of our highest purpose. Imagine that soul is an all-seeing guide, leading a visually impaired ego along a pathway. Soul can gently guide ego along what it sees as the best path. If ego is stubborn and persistent, it may override soul, insisting that it knows best.

Eventually ego stumbles. When that happens, ego can blame and judge others, or even curse the path. Further, ego may feel that the path is booby-trapped on purpose, just to make its life miserable.

Let us consider an example. Martin had trouble when he played high school football. He was a good athlete, but was not a team player. He often blamed teammates for failed plays, and when the coach called him on it, he felt unfairly singled out for criticism. Eventually he quit the team, saying he no longer wanted to play with 'a bunch of losers.'

In his personal life, he had several relationships before he married. They began intensely, but ultimately deteriorated into power struggles and arguing. When he was twenty-four, he married Jane, who was quite patient and forgiving. The marriage ended however, after four years. His wife found him to be controlling and critical, and despite counselling, he continued to blame her for the problems in the relationship.

Martin believed he was intelligent, strong, and could be a good leader if only people would listen to him, and see things his way. Indeed, he had ambition and was both bright and enthusiastic. These qualities allowed him to advance rapidly in his corporate job. Finally, he believed, he had reached a level where he could work with his equals: others who saw things the way he did, and could keep pace with his ideas.

He was devastated when he was first denied a promotion, and then told that his style no longer fit with the mission statement of the company. It seems they were looking for leaders who could work well with, and inspire others. Most importantly, they wanted someone who could make others feel heard, encouraging them to feel involved in moving the company forward.

Martin felt angry and betrayed. He blamed the CEO, suggesting the company only wanted 'yes men', and was disgusted that, yet again, he was foiled because others did not see things his way. Life is tough enough, but to be up against first a coach, then a wife, and now a company who 'sucked him in', only to later reject him, left Martin feeling bitter and resentful.

When he went for career counselling, the counsellor identified the recurring self-sabotaging patterns in his life. He began to understand how the 'self-centeredness' of his ego prevented him from seeing things from any other perspectives. He was a one-man dynamo all right! Unfortunately the dynamo destroyed many of the good things in his life. He was helped to see how his actions and behaviors affected others. Without this awareness, he may have continued running into walls, always blaming others for the outcomes he created.

Without awareness, ego continues trying to control, or fight against life. Crises are created, either triggering Dabrowski's process of positive adjustment described earlier, or resulting in a series of disasters. An awakening consciousness might begin to wonder why it keeps stumbling, and start thinking there must be a better way. Rather than bulldozing its way through the path, or withdrawing miserably into the bushes to feel sorry

The Continuum of Awareness and Behavior

for itself, the awakening consciousness, either spontaneously or with wise guidance, begins to reflect.

It is in this stopping to reflect that the energy of soul begins to be felt. It is felt first in the heart. The heart is the pathway through which soul speaks to us. In the midst of a conflict, the heart whispers that the experience is painful and distasteful to the organism.

When ego has distanced and closed itself off from a loved one, the heart yearns to be connected. A strong ego will attempt to block heart messages, as a parent of a teenager may disconnect the telephone to prevent the child from being influenced by others. A blocked heart hurts.

The individual feels it is others who have created the pain in their heart, while in truth it is self-created. A blocked heart does not permit the flow of love, and it is that flow of love that keeps one vibrant, healthy, alive and spirited. Love is healing, and the heart that is closed to love is closed to healing.

Without healing energy moving through the bodymind, the system is weakened. It is more vulnerable to illness, but particularly to anxiety and depression. Authors Pert, Pearsall, Ornish and Dreher have convincingly detailed the connections between thoughts and emotions, and physical and mental health.

We have described the way in which ego interprets the world. It judges situations or events in terms of polarity: good/bad, positive/negative, favorable/unfavorable. Ego's view is a limited, five-sensory, of-the-world interpretation, more appropriate for perceiving physical reality.

Soul interprets the world from what Gary Zukav, in his book *The Seat of the Soul,* calls a multi-sensory perspective. We could also say that the human who sees the world from a multi-sensory perspective is interpreting soul in the world. The multi-sensory perception is, as Zukav describes, a higher order of logic and understanding, which extends beyond physical reality to encompass the larger whole, of which physical reality is only a part. The soulful interpretation of the world, unlike the polarized view of ego, is characterized by understanding, compassion, and acceptance.

UNDERSTANDING

Soul is the all-knowing teacher. Soul watches the choices ego makes, sees the consequences, and observes the suffering. Imagine a very young child attempting to place various shaped puzzle pieces into their proper places. We show the child how it works, but it will take months before the child can do it correctly every time. Even if he has the right piece, he may not have the coordination to get it right, and may then assume it does not fit there. Similarly, he may persist in putting a wrong piece in a space because it almost fits. We watch the child practice, unconcerned with the rate of progress, knowing that learning takes time, and the child will eventually get it. From time to time we may assist the child, suggesting he try this one, or that one. After all, we want him to experience success!

In the same way, soul observes ego, and *understands* everyone is learning. It views difficult situations as opportunities for growth, and sees we are all participating in a process of co-creation. We each play a role in the learning opportunities of others, and they in ours. Soul looks at any situation in individual lives, or in the world community, and can see the learning that is playing itself out. It does not judge.

Soul sees the egos of others struggling to metamorphose into the lighter beings that can take flight, free of the weight and constraints of limited perceptions. If the ego (of self or other) is stuck, struggling painfully, unable to evolve, soul does not mock or belittle the one who 'just doesn't get it'.

Soul's response is compassion. Soul sends love, whether or not the troubled ego has blocked the heart, whether or not the love is consciously received. Soul, the all-knowing, beneficent teacher, wants success for all.

Consider the following example. One day as I was looking out of my upstairs window, I noticed the two girls who lived next-door playing on their swing set. The older one would have been about nine years old, the younger was six. I watched as the older one kept taunting and annoying the younger one. The younger sister told her repeatedly to stop, becoming increasingly frustrated. Upon seeing the frustration, the older one smiled and increased her taunting. Finally the younger one could take no more, pushed her sister away, and began screaming.

The mother ran out of the house, demanding to know what was going on. The older 'innocently' announced that the younger one had pushed her. The mother immediately began berating the young one, spanking her and sending her to her room.

The older one maintained a satisfied smile. This was a pattern that repeated itself many times, as the oldest protected her position as 'the good child', and did whatever she could to keep her sibling in the role of the 'bad child'.

Because the mother looked at things from a polarized point of view, it is not surprising that her children played this out. Always looking to find who was 'right' and who was 'wrong', the ego patterns in the mother's thinking became projected onto her children, who then lived those parts.

The parent coming from a soulful perspective would recognize that if the children are having difficulty with each other, *something else is going on.* The soulful *parent understands* that fights or squabbles between children occur because they do not have the strategies to deal with their own unconscious ego reactions. A small child cannot help it if he wants to play with the truck his brother just received as a present. The developing ego cannot be faulted for not welcoming the baby to the family, especially when it demands so much of Mom and Dad's attention, which previously was his, undivided.

The soulful parent *understands* that children need gentle guidance, and if they allow their own ego reactions to get in the way, they only strengthen the ego responses in their children. When we speak to children from our own hearts and souls, it activates their own inner soulfulness. Without awareness, we continue the old patterns, perpetuating the same struggles, conflicts, and polarities that have existed throughout the generations. Once we have the awareness of a soulful perspective, however, we have a choice.

COMPASSION

Compassion is the ability to see others as ourselves. When we can see that every human being is a mirror, reflecting back something of ourselves, we begin to feel what the other is feeling. We respond to others the way we would want others to respond to us. Compassion springs from an understanding of the interdependence and interconnectedness of all living things. To hurt another is to hurt ourselves. To heal another is to heal the world.

The essence of soul is compassion, springing from the awareness that, like drops in the ocean, we are all part of something much bigger. When we drop the boundaries imposed by ego, we re-experience oneness, as our energies reconnect with the larger, universal hologram. Every drop of ocean water retains its connection with the vast ocean. Every human soul retains its connection with the vast cosmos out of which it emerged. Compassion in life develops as human thought and action become more aligned with soul than with ego. Let us see how that happens.

The Continuum of Awareness and Behavior

In the process of evolving beyond the limited perceptions of ego, and expanding into the broader awareness of soul, there is much learning, struggle, and pain. Ego keeps bumping up against things that do not work. Ego tries hard, but sabotages itself again and again. Much as ego can be hard on others, it can be even harder on itself.

It is important to recognize that our egos are not 'bad'. They have outlasted their usefulness, however as the prime drivers of human awareness and behavior. Ego dominance may have been necessary for humans to survive and deal with the forces of nature.

Despite its valiant efforts to remain in power, a new order is emerging. Ego feels very lost and alone as it realizes it is losing its grip. It may respond with panic, and redouble its efforts to maintain control. It can do this for a very long time, creating more pain and chaos in life.

Like a stubborn child who refuses to hear what the wise parent is saying, ego plugs her ears, squeezes her eyes shut, and makes lots of her own noise to block out of her awareness the presence of any other viewpoint.

Soul understands how difficult it is for ego, and is always there as a compassionate presence. Compassion exists, at least in potential, in all people. It often becomes blocked early on, either because it is not modeled in our environment, or because ego consciousness fills the stage of our awareness. Even young children demonstrate compassion. If they happen to see Mom crying, you can almost feel their hearts opening as they offer a hug or a gentle pat on the hand. When they see new baby kittens, they automatically sense their vulnerability as they stumble around blindly looking for the source of nurturing. Adolescents often become passionate about certain causes, because they are enough in touch with their own pain to recognize pain in others.

Compassion differs from understanding in that it requires no thought. It is that pure knowing about what another is feeling. Like the children's game of trying to rub the stomach and pat the head at the same time, it is difficult to access compassion when the ego perspective is operating. As long as there is judgement, blame, criticism, or even ideas about who is right and who is wrong, there cannot be true compassion. Compassion is the ability to feel what another feels, *as though we were that person.* It requires stepping outside of ordinary thought.

I think about a minister and his wife who expressed forgiveness towards the young man who shot and killed their son in his school. Despite their own grief and loss, when put to the ultimate test, they still chose compassion for the troubled boy and his family.

The poet, Rumi, says that beyond all notions of right-doing and wrong-doing there is a field. "I'll meet you there," he offers. That is where compassion dwells. That field exists in each of us, and is fundamental to a soulful approach. Sometimes life events trigger our sense of compassion, forever changing us. Other times, our soul is touched, but then we consciously or unconsciously pass the reins back to ego. Soul watches, soul knows, soul waits for awareness.

It can be difficult enough developing compassion for others. Generally, however, compassion for our own selves, our learning process, our mistakes and limitations, is the most challenging task we face. Much as ego may have judged and criticized others, sometimes it is most persistent and damaging when it turns on the self.

Soul does not override ego; instead it waits patiently until ego becomes still, quiet, ready, and open. As long as ego retains control, it continues to attract life events, which contain the seeds of, or potential for, its own transformation. Like the seed buried in the ground, it has an inherent impetus for growth, slowly but surely stretching the boundaries that contain it.

Eventually that impetus results in a cracking or destruction of the outer shell. Without this 'falling apart' or disintegration of a once seemingly vital boundary, the miracle encoded within the seed could never become a blossom. Soul's energy is the ever-present, though at times dormant, impetus for human spiritual growth.

Just as the newborn, with appropriate nutrients, automatically evolves into an adult man or woman, so the human psyche was designed to automatically evolve into a more soulful expression of being. If physical growth is stunted, as when the ancient Chinese bound the feet of young girls, distortion occurs. If some seed jackets are not soaked and softened before planting, growth simply will not occur. Similarly, if humans are solidly identified with and entrenched in ego, personality becomes distorted, and growth of the psyche is stunted.

Our souls will support us as we work to free ourselves from the conditioning of ego. It is important to recognize and learn to access the comfort, support, and encouragement supplied endlessly by soul, for in transcending ego we will feel like we have lost our footing—like there is no solid ground beneath us. Taming ego can be a challenging and difficult process. Compassion for self and others is woven into the process, becoming part of the ultimate grand design. It becomes activated when we first have awareness, and then consciously choose the compassionate path.

ACCEPTANCE

A soulful interpretation of life events, which is grounded in understanding and compassion, results in an attitude of acceptance. Recall that soul does not judge things as good or bad.

Soul sees what is, and nods knowingly. Soul recognizes suffering as sometimes necessary: as with a woman giving birth, there may be pain and struggle, but it is because something important is occurring.

As parents watch a child learn from his or her mistakes, there is compassion for the pain, but they also see the value of the lesson. As humans become more aligned with the wisdom of their own souls, there is less of a resistance to what is unfolding in life. Rather than being attached to certain outcomes, there is a curious and reflective awareness about how we co-create outcomes with others and our world.

Like a baby who first watches the mobile go round and round, next discovers the effect of randomly batting it with a hand or foot, and finally forms a conscious intention to have an impact on a particular part of the mobile, humans go through a process of growing understanding about their ability to create results in the world.

The soulful perspective accepts that everyone is at a different place in his or her evolving awareness, and each is likely exactly where he or she needs to be at the moment. A new wisdom begins to emerge, so that things are no longer taken personally. Rather, there is acceptance that life events are simply challenges that provide continual opportunities to choose between ego-based or soul-based interpretations.

It is almost as though soul says to ego, "Smile, you're on candid camera! All of those frustrations were created for the sole (soul?) purpose of seeing how you would respond." Interestingly, on the *Candid Camera* TV program, we can see a wide range of reactions to frustrating or absurd situations. Some people get angry, some become frustrated or confused, and others regard the situation with humor.

As we move along the continuum from ego-based to soul-based interpretations and behaviors, there is a growing realization that what is important is not what happens to us, but how we respond. Therefore we begin to accept whatever comes as another challenge, another impetus which we can use to set ourselves back into ego-reaction, or to propel ourselves forward along soul's journey. The choice is ours.

AS WE INTERPRET, SO WE CREATE

When life happens to us, be it a turn of events, or an interaction with another, there is a point of intersection that is critical to what evolves next. It is the point, often beneath the level of conscious awareness, when we make a *choice* about how we will *interpret* that event.

If we align with ego, we immediately make a judgement, and respond according to that judgement. If it is a negative judgement, typical responses include blame, criticism, anger, withdrawal, or retaliation. If it is a positive judgement, responses may include joy, happiness, contentment, praise, or even love.

On the surface, such positive responses appear healthy. While appearing positive, it is still not healthy, for those good feelings do not exist independently within the being, but rather are a response to something outside ourselves. This means that the good feelings are conditional. We get them because the world has rewarded us in some way.

When the rewards are withdrawn, or simply do not come, there is pain, disappointment, or a sense of betrayal. Life is like a seesaw: sometimes we're up; sometimes we're down. Alignment with ego's interpretation results in certain qualities in our lives including polarity, adversarial situations, aggression, confrontation, resentment, punishment, and co-dependent relationships. Life, quite simply, becomes a struggle.

Alignment with soul interpretation, as described earlier,

Evolving Consciousness

Life Situation
⬇
Perceived Through Five Senses
⬇
Filtered Through
Genetic Predispositions - Past Experiences - Beliefs

⬇ Unconscious Reaction ⇅ Conscious Choice ⬆

Ego Interpretation of Situation ⟷ Soul Interpretation of Situation

Threatens Ego	**Understanding and Compassion**
Loss	Observes ego of self and others (Witness)
Rejection	See learning
Dissatisfaction	Sees opportunities for growth
Shame	Sees self in others (mirror)
Criticism	Identifies ego struggles
	See opportunities for healing

Acceptance
Universal perspective (wisdom)

Counter-Evolutionary Emotions and Behaviors	**Pro-Evolutionary Emotions and Behaviors**
Blame	Non-Attachment
Judgement	Unconditional Love
Confrontation	Independence
Polarity	Connectedness
Anger	Non-Judgmental
Jealousy	Helpfulness
Inferiority	Kindness
Hatred	Peace
Imbalance	Loving Connections
	Encouragement
	Trust
	Patience
	Allowing
	Openness
	Freedom
	Contentment
	Harmony
	Serenity

Feeds Ego
Personal Gain
Approval
Winning
Pride
Validation

Attachment
Greed
Superiority
Selfishness
Manipulation
Competition
Control
Co-Dependency
Struggle

See diagram 2 for life consequences of reaction vs. conscious choice Diagram 1

Copyright Gwen Randall-Young 2004

Evolving Consciousness

Ego-Based Interpretation of Life	Soul-Based Interpretation of Life
⇒ Leads to ⇒	⇒ Leads to ⇒
Life Characterized By:	**Life Characterized By:**
Contracted energy (low energy)	Expansive energy (high energy, synergy)
Tense approach to life	Relaxed approach to life
Self-esteem issues	Self-validation
Anxiety	Balanced mood
Depression	Elimination of anger reactions
Anger issues	Release of addictive behaviors
Addictions	Healthy communication
Blocked creativity	Increased creativity
Communication problems	Effective problem resolution skills
Conflict with family	Mutually respectful family relations
Relationship Struggles	Satisfying intimate relationships
Conflict in the workplace	Mature responses to workplace issues
Financial issues	Financial responsibility
Compromised Physical and Emotional Health	Physical and emotional vitality

Ego-Based Living .... Evolutionary Continuum of Consciousness .... Soul Based Living

Copyright Gwen Randall-Young 2004

Diagram 2

results in a significantly different set of qualities. Recall that soul interpretation is based on understanding, compassion, and acceptance. Because these qualities are inherent in our soul essence, they are not dependent on anything outside of ourselves. They are self-perpetuating and enduring.

As we interpret, so we create. This is true for individuals, and it holds true globally. If we think of the continuum with the more primitive ego-consciousness at one end, and the more evolved soul-consciousness at the other, the individual who functions closer to the ego end of the continuum creates pain, and struggle in his life. The individual who functions closer to the soul end creates balance and contentment in his life.

Globally, the closer to the ego end of the continuum we function as a civilization, the more war, conflict, and aggression we create. The closer to the soul end of the continuum we function as a civilization, the more harmony, co-operation, and reverence for all life we create.

The diagrams on the previous pages allow us to see at a glance how our choice of perspective generates radically different outcomes.

The following chapters will include common real life situations that demonstrate very specifically the principles described above. We will see the impact and outcome of ego-based interpretations.

Practical suggestions and strategies will be provided to demonstrate how we can move ourselves further along the continuum in the direction of soul-consciousness. The strategies presented may sometimes feel awkward and unnatural, for they are not the way we have been conditioned by ego. We may feel as though we have lost control completely, and will be tempted to go back to the old way—and we *will*, again and again. Each time, however, we will see once more how the old ways create the old patterns.

The Continuum of Awareness and Behavior

Those with whom we interact may be confused when we begin a new approach. At first *they* may respond in the old way, for *their* egos are more comfortable with the familiar. When we come from soul with those who have only seen our egos, there may be distrust, even mockery. Others may think we are simply trying to manipulate them, and that we will not sustain our attitude of caring and compassion.

Our challenge is to remain centered in soul-knowing, despite invitations to abandon it. By being true to our souls, we may awaken the soul consciousness in others. That is precisely what we all came here to do for each other. It is the most important journey we will ever take, and like all-important journeys, it requires some preparation. For this one, however, the preparation is internal. The next chapter will explain this process in detail.

Chapter 4

PREPARATION FOR THE JOURNEY

GETTING READY FOR CHANGE

In this chapter we will create a bridge between the more abstract, philosophical concepts relevant to the kind of change upon which the evolving human is embarking, and the more concrete concepts that apply directly to each one of us on an individual level.

We are all participants on this journey along the continuum of evolutionary growth. Where we are on the path, and the quality of our lives, will be determined by the level of awareness we bring to the process. Intellectual understanding is not enough. In fact, many are frustrated by the fact that they 'know' so much, but simply cannot consistently apply their knowing when it comes to the practical situations which arise daily.

The most difficult aspect of any path of transformation is the shift from 'knowing', to 'doing', to 'being'. First we 'know' the way, then we begin practice, or 'doing', based on the knowing, and ultimately we *become* the way. That is to say, *we become a living example of the highest principles we have been holding in consciousness.*

Imagine, that for this evolutionary journey, we have all entered a magnificent spacecraft that will take us along the path. In truth we have. The wondrous spacecraft is planet Earth. Perhaps, if this process were depicted in a Star Trek episode, over a universal intercom, the following message might be broadcast:

Attention all passengers on Planet Earth. Your evolutionary program requires a course adjustment at this time. You must activate your super-conscious universal hologram system, which is located in your over-head compartment. This will permit you to receive incoming messages, as well as to access all facets of cosmic intelligence. Your flight locator, situated in your chest cavity compartment must be maintained in the open position at all times, so that other passengers carrying vital flight plan information will gravitate towards you and have required access to your flight plan input system. Failure to activate these systems will result in unnecessary delays, missed connections, and severe underutilization of your universal holographic info-net. Should you choose non-activation, you will remain at your current consciousness altitude and vibratory frequency for the remainder of this lifetime. You may now unfasten your seatbelts and prepare for transcendence. Have a pleasant flight.

TWO BASIC PRINCIPLES

There are two principles that are fundamental to making such a critical course adjustment:

1) *You cannot carry the past into the future.* This kind of travel is different from travelling on Earth. No map is required, as the flight plan has been pre-programmed at both cellular and non-physical levels. Previous experience is not required and may be irrelevant, or a hindrance. As the flight moves through alternative dimensions of consciousness (along the continuum from ego to soul consciousness), the carrying of any baggage is discouraged.

   Once past events are recognized as opportunities for growth, and the learning has been taken from them, forward progress requires that they be released. Past, present, and future are like time zones: you cannot be in two simultaneously. You must be in motion in order to move from one zone to another. Changing time zones requires physical movement. Shifting along the continuum to a new dimension of awareness requires movement: it requires expansion of our very perception of our own consciousness.

2) *It is our perception that needs to expand.* Saying that consciousness needs to expand in order to understand more is like saying that the Earth needs to expand so that you can have a bigger house. Imagine that consciousness is already huge: that there is a cosmic intelligence that is beyond human comprehension. We can tune into it, but it is not 'knowable' through ordinary thinking.

   Cosmic intelligence may be likened to a hard drive

in your computer. It holds all the programs, including the program for running the programs. Unless you are a programmer with a huge knowledge base, you only know what the programs do, not why or how they do it. No single computer programmer could possibly 'know' all the programs that currently exist in the world.

The 'cosmic programmer' developed every existing program in all of the universes, from galaxies to hummingbirds, from magnetic fields to a baby's giggle. The Universe has been described as holographic, the whole existing in every part. Physicist David Bohm, and neurologist Karl Pribram postulate the brain as a hologram interpreting this holographic universe.

The Universe, and the mind that knows the Universe are a connected whole. Thus, it is our *perceptions* that need to expand to embrace a larger view of what the cosmos might be about. It is certainly too large to wrap our minds around, but we can, in a multitude of ways, explore many parts and the wholeness within each. Everyday experience provides myriad keyholes through which to glimpse fragments of the mysterious, magnificent and Divine whole, of which *you* are an important part.

These principles are profoundly important in the journey from ego-based living to soul-based living. It is hard to implement them without fully understanding them. Let us look a little closer.

OF WHAT SIGNIFICANCE ARE PAST EXPERIENCES?

Some struggle with the idea of leaving the past behind. It seems too important, too relevant, or even too painful to simply discard. Leaving the past behind does not mean forgetting it completely, or discounting its significance. What it does mean is understanding the impact of the past, and integrating it into who we are becoming. Consider some examples.

The gifted artist may once have spent hours gazing at a colorful mobile in his crib, and perhaps scribbled on the walls with his crayons. The musician, as a child, may have been soothed by music, or the sound of her mother singing. Perhaps she was entranced by the sound the lid made as she banged it against the pot. The empathic therapist may have spent years as a child experiencing pain, loneliness and fear.

A plant begins as a seed in darkness under the ground. It must begin to germinate, and then it must push its way up towards the light. Where, in that germinating seed, are the colorful blossoms that will one day burst forth in exquisite expression of color, form and fragrance? Where, but in potential?

A human also begins as a fertilized egg, germinating in darkness, and life is movement in the direction of unfolding potential. It could be said that past experiences are no more relevant to the unfolding of potential than the weather conditions at the time of initial planting are to a blossom on a mature rose bush.

Certainly past experiences affect our development, but once we awaken to a new understanding of consciousness, the past is nothing more than a condition that existed long ago. Once we understand how it might have affected us within the context of our limited perceptions, and whatever limiting beliefs we may have formulated in reaction to it, then it is time to move on. A rose is most lovely when it reaches up towards the sky, into the light, not when it leans over contemplating the earth from which it came, and in which it is rooted.

This is not to say we should totally disregard the past. If there is something there that hinders or blocks expression of potential, then it needs to be cleared. You shovel snow from the driveway so that you can get the car out and get on with your day. You don't put it in the car trunk and take it everywhere you go. The same is true of the past: it is enough to recognize and understand what it is, to move it aside, allowing it to eventually melt away.

EXPANDING PERCEPTION: WE ARE MOVING TOWARDS THE LIGHT

We live on a planet that rotates, as it travels in an orbit within a galaxy, in a Universe that is hurtling through space. How many universes might there be, and what is the super-universe that contains them all? What does *it* move through? And how many of *those* might there be? Even if we cannot answer these questions, we know that movement and change are constants. We are reaching a stage in our evolution where we are emerging from the dark soil of limited awareness and are just beginning our upward journey towards the light of an infinitely more expansive awareness.

We will blossom into a new kind of being as different from who we are now, as the rose blossom is from the first shoot that emerged from the soil. Each stage in our growth is a necessary precondition for the next stage. That is why we have needed to be where we were at any given time. How could we become enlightened if a state of non-enlightenment did not pre-exist?

Everything is happening exactly as it needs to be. A great awakening is occurring on our planet; if you were not also awakening you would not be reading this. Provided in these pages is a blueprint for accessing your own unlimited power, wisdom, and knowledge. However, as in learning to float on your back in the water, you must first surrender and let go of the old ways before you are free to be, in a new way.

LIVING A PARADOX: WE ARE PREPROGRAMMED, *AND* WE ARE THE CREATORS OF OUR OWN LIVES

It has been said that truth lies at the heart of the paradox. There is an order and a purpose to all life on Earth—a natural unfolding that at times seems incredibly perfect. It is hard to imagine such a Divine game could have been designed with an interactive component. Perhaps the creator wanted to make it more interesting, or maybe life is the ultimate programmed learning experience. Whatever the case, we *do* have a choice, and we can utilize our minds to create change in the same way that we use a remote control to change the television channel.

If we do not like a given situation, we can leave the situation, change it, or look at it in a different way. Whichever we choose, our reality changes. A miracle has been described as a shift in perception. Victor Frankl, author of *Man's Search for Meaning,* shifted his perception to survive life in a concentration camp. Perceptions are shifting in regard to nuclear arms, environmental consciousness, health and healing. First comes the shift in perception, and then the reality begins to change. Without a shift in perception, things go on as before.

Shifts in perception manifest within the consciousness of individuals, initially one by one. When a critical mass is reached, awareness seems to spread in an all-at-once way: everyone just 'knows'. There are myriad programs operating within individuals, like a mass of highways and interchanges. If you are not thinking about where you are going, you could drive forever without running out of road. It could *seem* that your path is pre-determined.

A higher level of awareness would involve recognition that other roads exist. The next stage would be to learn where those other roads lead. Then you are in a position to begin to make conscious choices. In every area of life there are similar levels of awareness. They can be visualized as the rings of an upward spiral, with the lowest point being a state of total egocentricity—awareness only of self. Ideally, throughout life, we would move ever further to expanded levels of awareness, seeing life from continually broadening perspectives. The more we are able to transcend the limited perspective of ego-consciousness, the more whole and integrated we become.

Imagine we are like snowflakes. Before actual snowflakes come into form, they exist as potential in the ethereal atmosphere. With the right conditions, what was once invisible and only a possibility, takes on physical form. Snowflakes are real, incredibly complex, each different from any other. We can melt them on our tongues, build snowmen with them, or ski on them. Eventually their form changes, they begin to melt away, evaporate, and return to the energy field from which they came.

Like snowflakes, we once existed as potential, and then took on physical form; we are real, complex and unique. One day we too, will return to the energy field out of which we came. The day we are born we enter into physical form, and the day we die we leave that form behind.

The sooner we release our attachment to ego-consciousness and begin identifying more with our soulful nature, the easier it will be to make that transition. We are continually in a process of transition, *whether we are aware of it or not.* Becoming attached to the physical manifestation of our being, and the ego-interpretation of who we are, ultimately will result in pain, because that is what happens when we want to hold on to something that is transient. The fear around losing our 'self' can be so great that we continue to fortify that self, building and expanding upon it, creating our place in the world, burying our heads deeper and deeper into the sands of unconsciousness.

We validate and reinforce each other's ego perceptions. Like the people in the fairy tale about the emperor's new clothes, we all share the pretence that what we imagine life to be is real. We blindly ignore the fact that we have been building elaborate lives on a foundation of impermanence. Eventually we face a growing uneasiness as we realize we are not completely in control. We cannot control the passage of time, nor can we stop change. There is a bigger program than the one we have created for ourselves.

What we *can* control is the way in which we understand or interpret this journey of life. To view it simplistically, as 'you are born, you live, you die', is to miss the elegance, the complexity, and the beauty of the experience. The body was designed to grow physically according to some inner clockwork, and it does just that. Consciousness grows as well. The adult understands so much more than the child, but the process does not mysteriously stop at adulthood any more than does the body stop changing.

The process of growth in consciousness is one of making shifts from one level of awareness up or out to the next. These shifts can come through reflection, but are more likely triggered by events or situations in our lives. We can become aware of these levels in our understanding of relationships, business, emotions, and spirituality: in virtually every area of life.

Because we live in an expanding universe, and because our consciousness is our experience of the Universal intelligence, there is no upper limit to awareness. No one could claim to be totally evolved any more than one could claim to know everything. This is not a static universe. There is a flow that carries us, and we create a flow within that flow, co-creating with the Universe our very experience of her.

THE PROCESS OF EXPANDING AWARENESS CAN BE ENHANCED

In the same way that we can utilize a wide variety of methods to get our bodies in good physical shape, there are a multitude of approaches to exercising our awareness; there are many paths from which to choose. These paths include meditation, yoga, prayer, bodywork, breathwork, reading, swimming with dolphins, travel, and art, to name only a few. Certain practices may not be helpful for some individuals because they do not appeal, or because the individual is not ready. There may be different paths for some people at different times in their lives. Some dedicate their lives to a formal and disciplined practice, believing we cannot transcend the limited ego-mind without doing so.

Formal practice is not necessarily required, as any activity can be consciousness expanding if it is performed with reverence. I once knew an elderly gentleman who planted a little garden each year, and tending to it was his meditation. Each year he saved the seeds from one tomato, and planted them the following year. He participated in co-creating the process and continuity of life in a very simple, yet profound way. People can spend year after year practicing meditation and still not grow. Or, they can form the intention to see more deeply, and do so in an instant. It is more about letting go of attachment to old ways of seeing things, than it is about learning something new.

Think of the three-dimensional computer generated 'magic-eye' pictures that look like a mass of lines, but have a picture embedded within. Trying 'hard' to see the image makes it more elusive. Relaxing the eyes, and simply letting the image emerge is the effortless way. The image is there all the time—we only have to let ourselves see it. A higher level of consciousness awareness is also there, just waiting to be perceived. It does not have to be difficult.

It is said there are certain 'power spots' on the Earth where the energy facilitates the opening process in attuned individuals. There are also visionary artists and writers whose work stretches the boundaries of our consciousness. Exposure to such places and works can certainly speed up the process. Anything that assists us in quieting the mind, creating an inner receptivity, invites us to see what has been there all the time, just out of range of our attention. It is possible to drive all the way home, lost in thought, seeing nothing of what is around you, and in fact, having no remembrance of how you even got home. This is the way many go through life, perhaps waking up at fifty years old, or thirty or eighty, and wondering where they have been all those years.

It is time now for *everyone* to come out of that trance. In the past, the mystics, philosophers and gurus did their own searching, and shared in their own language with their followers. There is so much that has been written that is beautiful and profound in its teaching. If you have the time and the inclination, you too could devote yourself to a path of enlightenment. You could take workshops, join ashrams, or go to live in a monastery. Many have done these things, and prepared the soil for a new crop of perceivers.

The time of great transformation for which these people have been preparing is now upon us. It is no longer sufficient for select groups here and there to access the expansive cosmic intelligence. It is important for individuals and the species to learn how to incorporate cosmic intelligence into daily life.

In the following chapters you will be shown, through direct examples and simple language, how to begin a powerful process of transformation. The beauty of the process is that as you practice, the underlying, profound insights will reveal themselves to you, as surely as the crocuses emerge from beneath the snow with the coming of spring.

IF IT IS SO SIMPLE, WHY IS LIFE A STRUGGLE?

Remember, we are an evolving species. The human journey has been one of transformation and mastery. In cosmic terms, it was not long ago that the Earth was perceived to be the center of the Universe—and flat, at that.

I am aware of the struggle my grandmother endured when she came to Canada in the early 1900's. The first task was to clear the land. It is never easy for the pioneers, and their entire lifetime may be spent on mastery of some sort in the physical realm. Learning how to survive in terms of food, clothing and shelter has been, and continues to be the major concern of mankind. In the past, those whose lives were not taken up with concerns of physical survival, or those who had relinquished materialism, were free to explore other realms of human perception. There was no particular urgency or need for everyone to get on the same track.

However, as Jonas Salk explained in his book, *Survival of the Wisest,* the values and characteristics that allowed humans to survive and master the physical world during the first "half" of the growth curve of our civilization, would have to shift if we were to survive and thrive in the second half. There would need to be an inversion in values: away from aggression, competition and strictly analytical thinking, towards cooperation and synthesis. We have seen these shifts in many aspects of life, and what we know is that where the old values are still held, struggle and pain result. Where there is no reverence for the Earth, her forests are destroyed and her waters are poisoned. Where there is no reverence for life, people are being massacred. On the level of individual lives, those who resist aligning with the new values will experience frustration, conflict, and compromised emotional and physical health.

Whenever there is struggle in our lives, it means that we are holding on to limiting beliefs or feel a need to control something. Like the monkey with the hand in the cookie jar, who can neither enjoy his cookies nor get free as long as he clutches them tightly, people remain stuck, wishing somehow that their situation would change. We struggle because we do not realize that on some level we are *creating* the struggle. Usually, relief can be obtained by letting go. The next chapter will show, quite simply, those qualities and behaviors we need to leave behind as we move into a new way of being. To free the soul, we must let go of all that chains it.

Chapter 5

MOVING FORWARD— RELEASING THE OLD

Certain attributes and ways of thinking no longer serve us, and will actually prevent growth. These include *polarity, aggression, anger, fear, the need to be right, the need to control, denial,* and *the false self.*

POLARITY

Polarity results from thinking in terms of opposites. Mine/yours, right/wrong, good/bad, and win/lose, are polar opposites. While there are certainly times when we need to set boundaries based on these poles, we need to begin looking more and more at those places where polarizing creates more problems than it solves. There is nothing wrong with seeing a situation differently from someone else: it is when we say (or think) we are right and they are wrong that the trouble starts.

There is rarely much to be gained in trying to convince someone that they are wrong. It is much better to acknowledge that you both see things differently, respect the other's view, and focus on where to go from there. Given that I see it this way, and you see it that way, what solutions exist? Focusing on creatively resolving polarity is one way we grow into our higher selves.

AGGRESSION

Aggression is a biological response to a life-threatening situation. When there is an immediate threat to life, aggressive energy provides the power to do what needs to be done. Aggression in normal daily interactions is like activating a smoke alarm when there is no smoke. Actually, it is worse. The ringing alarm would be annoying, but it would do no harm. Aggression at best is annoying, and at worst, itself, becomes life threatening.

Aggressive energy is a lower form of energy, and acts like emotional or psychological pollution. If you have an aggressive outburst, your body does not feel good. Being aggressive might get you your way in the short term, but no short-term gain is worth the long-term damage to your body and to your relationships.

Aggression is different from anger. Anger is an emotion; aggression is a behavior. There are better ways to deal with anger than behaving aggressively. Aggressive talk, gestures or behaviors belong to the old way of being. Once we tune in to a higher level of consciousness, aggression is as unnecessary as is the hand-held plow in modern day agriculture.

ANGER

Anger is an emotional response based on one's interpretation of a situation. Even if only at a subconscious level, judgement precedes anger. Notice what happens in a movie theater. If a 'good guy' gets shot, there is quiet outrage in the audience. If a 'bad guy' gets shot, there is often cheering. If someone cuts you off in traffic, you might be angry. If the ambulance driver cuts someone off while rushing your injured child to the hospital, you are grateful.

Anger is a result of how we interpret the intentions of another, or the situation. It can also result from a mismatch between what ego wants to happen, and what actually happens. Anger is very much an ego-driven emotion. Anger has a purpose biologically, in that it increases adrenaline levels, facilitating the fight or flight response.

Outside of threatening situations, the energy of anger is often toxic. If expressed as aggression, it can result in inappropriate or ineffective behaviors. If held inside, it can produce bitterness, resentment, depression, and a host of stress related health problems.

Anger is often blamed on the behaviors of others, when in reality it is a signal to ourselves that we are not using effective strategies in dealing with certain situations. It is a sign that ego's strategies are not working, and we must tune into our higher wisdom to assess what is really going on in our lives.

FEAR

Like anger, fear serves a useful purpose in protecting the human organism from life threatening situations. It allows us to avoid danger, or to mobilize our energy to protect ourselves or escape.

Ego, however, draws inappropriately on the body's emergency response system to protect and defend its own agendas. Ego constantly fears not getting what it wants, or losing what it has accumulated, be it love, admiration, or material possessions. Ego's biggest fear is losing control of its own domain (the self), others, or the external situation. Consequently, ego's fears drive it to control, even if that requires manipulation or intimidation. Since ego defines itself in terms of things external, it is always vulnerable, for there is just too much beyond its control.

When we shift to a soulful perspective, we release that need to control. To the extent we can release it, our fears diminish. If we love ourselves unconditionally, that inner balance is not threatened if we lose a job, friendship, relationship, or even a physical capability. We might feel sadness, regret, or disappointment, but since we realize some things simply are what they are, we do not live in fear about what we might one day lose. Ego grasps tightly. Soul is not attached to outcomes or things. Moving along the continuum towards soul-based living means learning to let go of control, to let go of expectations, and to have understanding, acceptance, and compassion for ourselves and for others, no matter what happens.

THE NEED TO BE RIGHT

We are all at different places in our journey along the continuum from ego-based to soul-based living, and it is not for us to try to control or judge the path of another person. To feel that our way is the right way, or that we are more evolved than someone else, is to take a judgmental stance. We cannot truly do our own work while directing our attention towards the improvements we think someone else needs to make. Whenever we judge another, we are being shown a place in ourselves that is still in darkness. Judging another says more about us than it does about the other. When we feel smug and correct, we may only be admiring the closed doors of our own hearts and minds.

There is a pattern and a connectedness to all things. Separateness is an illusion. When we do not see the oneness, it is we who are doing the separating or fragmenting. A small infant holding a rattle might see first one end, then the other, not realizing they are connected, or that he *holds* the connection. *We* can become the link between polarized positions, joining and connecting them, illuminating the wholeness like a symphony conductor bringing all of the parts into a harmonious whole. This is how we bring peace into our lives, and ultimately, to the world.

THE NEED TO CONTROL

The need to control produces struggle. Certainly there are times when we must exert control, for example, when the safety of a child is at stake. We can also set boundaries indicating our limits in various situations and relationships. We create difficulty though, when we try to control the thoughts, feelings or behavior of others. We also create struggle when we *need* things to turn out in a certain way. Ego decides it can only be happy if we get that job, car, house or date. If it does not happen that way, various degrees of misery can result.

People will go to great lengths to manipulate individuals and situations to get what they want, forgetting that agendas based on the wants or needs of others, or on a Divine plan, may be operating as well. If we force the outcome *we* want, it is unlikely the joy of attainment will be long-lived. If a partner leaves, or the promotion does not come, it may be because our true path (based on the wisdom of the soul) lies in a different direction. Sometimes the "worst" thing that could happen ultimately turns out to be the best thing that could have happened.

In letting go of the need to control, we allow ourselves to flow with what is: to be carried by the current rather than fighting against it. This does not mean becoming completely passive. Rather, it means utilizing the natural forces of the Universe to carry us in the direction of our dreams. The catch is that we have to let the Universe, as intuited and expressed through soul, have some input into what those dreams will be. If we insist on being in control, we turn our backs on a huge resource. If we work with the Universal energy, we can allow the miracles to emerge.

DENIAL

Denial is an ego defense mechanism, a kind of psychological camouflage that prevents one from seeing the truth of one's own situation. It is different from denying a truth. Denying is knowing, but covering up. With denial, the subconscious effectively blocks awareness, so the individual truly does not see the truth. A businessman might be in denial about the health of his business, despite declining profits. A woman might be in denial about her husband's affair because she does not want it to be happening and fears if she talks about it, he'll leave. Most smokers are in denial about the hazards to their health. Parents might be in denial about the fact that the way they are raising their children is just not working. It is easier to blame the children.

Being in denial stunts our growth. It is a way of escaping truth and seemingly taking the easy way out—but that is like seeing the automobile gas gauge on empty and ignoring it because you do not want to stop and fill up. Sooner or later life forces us out of our denial. The businessman finds that the bank has closed his line of credit. The unfaithful husband asks for a divorce. The smoker gets lung cancer. The teenagers get into drugs or run away from home. Those who were in denial go into shock, wondering how this could have happened to them.

Letting go of denial may be one of the most difficult aspects of growth, because it means really seeing truth, and dealing with it; yet it also has the power to be one of the most transformative aspects of this journey. Simply having the courage to acknowledge what you know in your heart is true, and bringing it out into the open with the intention of consciously creating a higher level of integrity in the situation, is enough to begin a process of positive change. This process can feel threatening or filled with risk, and you may need guidance or support in first becoming clear in your own mind about what is true for you. A clarifying question to ask yourself is whether the situation is serving the highest good of all concerned. If it is not serving the highest good of *all,* it is not serving the highest good of any. A situation that is dishonest, unhealthy, or unsatisfying does not serve anyone. Making a shift may feel like ripping off a bandage, but exposure to clarity and truth is healing.

FALSE SELF

False self is an aspect of ego: the personality which many, if not most, project out into the world. We have been conditioned to put on certain faces when we leave home. Examples might be the good student, team player, macho man, super mom, cool dude, or sharp executive. Putting on a front in certain situations serves ego, but violates soul if we *become so identified with it that we negate our real feelings and who we truly are.* If we create a false image, then we are not living authentically. Life becomes a struggle in which it is difficult to relax and let down our guard. Some have done this all their lives, and do not know their own essence. They are busy with life, but do not know who they really are deep down. Some are afraid to look inside, because they fear they may not like who they are—or worse yet, afraid if they look inside they may find no one there.

The most important step in releasing these attributes that fulfill only ego-needs, is to be aware that we have them. This is not as easy as it sounds. It can be difficult to recognize these features in our own personalities. Denial may prevent us from seeing when we are in polarity, controlling, taking an aggressive stance, or when we are more focused on being right than being happy. We can be pretty certain that if we are experiencing conflict and struggle with the people or situations in our lives, on some level these ego attributes are still operative. Releasing them is a process of surrender, and it is humbling.

They may never be released completely, for once and for all, for the path of growth is an upward spiral. Just when we think we are free and clear of old patterns, it seems we are tested at a higher level. Career, relationship and finances may all be in order, and just when you begin to relax into the feeling of success in life, perhaps delving more into personal growth, your children become adolescents, and may challenge everything you stand for. They can push every button you are aware of, and some you did not know you had. Ego can kick in again pretty fast.

Often I see couples where one partner has embarked on a 'spiritual' path, and appears to be evolving quickly. They are drawn to the positive principles, and work to incorporate them into their life. One day they notice they have moved 'way ahead' of their partner, and are frustrated because he or she 'just doesn't get it'. Before long they are judging, criticizing and blaming the 'unevolved' partner for the problems in the relationship. They have fallen right back into the old ego interpretation without even realizing it. When I gently point out that the way they are treating their partner does not seem very 'spiritual' to me, they often sit in stunned silence. Ego has a way of sneaking back in like that, even when we are on a spiritual path.

If we are aware and open, we can be thankful for those situations that reflect back to us where we are stuck. If we are humbled by those experiences, it is a good sign. It means that we are becoming uncomfortable with our ego interpretations and reactions. As the discomfort increases, the motivation for releasing them becomes stronger. As when cleaning out a closet, it is easier to get rid of things we know we will never want to be seen in again.

IF I LET GO, WHO WILL I BE?

It can be unsettling to release ways of being that have been part of our repertoire of beliefs and behaviors for a lifetime, whether they were held consciously or unconsciously. For some, it seems like giving up power, and there is the fear others will overpower or take advantage of us. Some feel the changes will leave them vulnerable and exposed. It is quite normal to wonder about the person into whom you will evolve.

You will still be the unique and precious being you have always been, but letting go of the habits which create struggle will allow the turbulent waters around you to become still, so that you can see your clear reflection. Your worth does not come from anything, or anyone outside of yourself. It has nothing to do with how popular or wealthy you are, or what others think of you.

A flower is beautiful simply because it is what it is. You are important and worthy simply because you are you. Unhappiness and disappointment in life are directly proportional to the unhappiness and disappointment we feel in ourselves. We must not judge ourselves, for when we do, we alienate ourselves from our essence. Unhappiness, disappointment, and judgment are the ego evaluating itself. Our consciousness cannot be with ego and soul at the same time. If we are judging, we are in ego-consciousness, hence disconnected from soul awareness.

If *our behavior* is not serving us or the world, we can see that and change it. Pain is the indicator that change is needed. If we resist change, or do not know how to change, pain and struggle increase. If we flow with, and put our energy into positive change, we learn, grow, and evolve. The *choice* is ours.

If struggle continues, we are at some level *choosing* it, even if only by *not choosing* to change the way we see and respond to life. We are here to learn to love and honor ourselves, for that is to honor life and all that is. We are a part of the whole, no lesser or greater than any other part. The Universe is not hierarchical: there is no cosmic pecking order. We are part of the shifting kaleidoscopic pattern that continually creates itself anew. The shifting patterns are the dance of the soul, and the soul needs no permission, no adornment, no effort. It is perfect just as it is, where it is, and how it is. If change is to happen for the soul, it will come from the dance. The energy for the dance comes through love, and until we can truly love and honor our own essence as a part of the miracle of creation, we do not know love, and we have not entered the dance.

ACCESSING TRUE SELF

I am often asked how one goes about locating and engaging the true self. When we have been on automatic pilot for so long, we forget how to master our own controls. Fortunately, we have a built-in, intuitive compass to show us the way. But we have to learn to tune in to it. This involves really listening to the heart. We have tended to be far more connected to our heads, particularly when it comes to making decisions. The heart may try to get a word in edgewise, but the head often overrules.

Imagine that your true path is a smooth, shiny metal road, and that your heart is a powerful magnet. When you are far from your path, the energy of attraction—be it to your job, partner, or geographical location, for example—is very weak. When you are near to your true path, or even thinking about it, there is a very powerful attraction or connection. The true self is that heart-knowing which is always there beneath the chatter of the mind. It is frequently expressed in intuition, and recognized most often after the fact, when we say, "I *knew* I should have..." or, "I had a *feeling* that...".

True self exists and expresses itself beneath the level of language. When we have a feeling or an experience that is indescribable, it does not mean we do not have an adequate vocabulary, but rather that the true self is bigger than words. True self is moved to tears. Ego blinks them back. True self would like to pay a compliment. Ego self stops, wondering how it will sound. True self wants to say, "I'm sorry," and end the argument. Ego self says, "Why should I be the one to do that?" True self *knows* if you hate your job and if it is unhealthy for you to stay in it, but ego self tells you to keep on plugging. True self *knows* that you should not yell at the kids, run the red light, or cheat on taxes. No wonder ego self tries to drown it out. It takes less effort to remain unconscious.

You can experiment with accessing the voice of true self by holding in consciousness several possible options that exist for you in any situation, then tune into your heart, and see which option tugs it most strongly. You can try this with major decisions, or something as simple as how to spend your Saturday. Once you have begun to tune in to your heart knowing, whenever possible follow its lead. To the extent that you can do this you will be living in true self. You must be careful to discern if the head is drowning out the heart. Put your attention in your heart, going to that place where there are no words. If you are tuning in to a debate or lecture, you are *not* in your heart.

People are often afraid to listen to their hearts, because they fear they will *have* to act, ending their relationship or quitting their job. This is not the case. You can tune in to your heart many, many times before finally deciding to take some action, if necessary. It is a process of deepening our awareness of what genuinely feels right, congruent, and integrated with all of who we truly are. Keeping a journal can also help to enhance your perception of true self, because if you are not being honest in your writing, the incongruity is as glaring as a spelling mistake.

Nurturing the true self is like preparing the soil for planting. What grows in well-prepared and enriched soil is both qualitatively and quantitatively different from what comes from poor soil. Understanding of, and connection with, soul and higher self comes most clearly through a well-developed and integrated true self.

In the next chapters we will begin to look at concrete examples demonstrating the character of ego consciousness, and how soul consciousness can change the process and outcomes in all areas of life.

Chapter 6

LOVE:
A SOULFUL PERSPECTIVE

THE FORCE THAT CONNECTS

There is a binding energy that holds everything in the Universe in place: things are attracted towards one another, yet remain in a state of balance. Scientists can study this force and its effects, but as yet we do not understand that attracting energy itself. Brian Swimme, cosmologist, uses the term *allurement*, to describe the forces of attraction which exist on all levels of being. The word some use for this fundamental dynamic is love.

However you define it, there is a *life force* that keeps things going. Love, attraction, allurement: it is what brought the Universe into being, what created life, what caused your ancestors to live where they lived, move where they moved, and to reproduce. You are a product of this chain of allurements. Love is not something that *began* for you the day you were born, or that you were taught to do or feel. You were born both out of, and into, that flow of energy that drives the Universe, and which underlies and infuses all of life. It exists on many levels. In our own bodies, and within our own consciousness, we feel it as love: love for ourselves, love for others, love for the world.

EGO, SOUL AND LIFE FORCE

The soul is in perfect alignment and harmony with that underlying life force. In fact, we can think of soul almost as a personification of that energy. It is how, and where that energy manifests within us.

Ego's focus is narrower, perceiving this energy only in relation to itself. Ego tries to 'stake a claim' on some of this territory. It is a little like the differing views about land ownership. Many Native people think it strange that anyone would claim ownership of land; they see the Earth as a living organism shared by all who live here. Throughout history, however, ego-driven humans have tended to 'stake their claims', and defined territory and borders, which then became the focus of disputes, battles and wars. Likewise, ego wants to 'own' or hold on to parcels of the love, or life force, which is everywhere. It wants to get some for itself, perhaps even to hoard it.

Soul, on the other hand, recognizes abundance and sufficiency, and flows in a relaxed, expansive manner. Fearing scarcity, ego contracts into holding, possessing, and attempting to protect itself from loss. Instead of relaxing into a state of love, allowing the loving energy of the Cosmos to flow through its being and out towards others, ego wants to grab on and hold what it can for itself. Let us look at what this means in terms of daily living.

CHILDHOOD EXPERIENCES OF LOVE

If we go back to the beginning, early in the life of a child, we find that children raised by parents who are unconditionally loving and accepting tend to be open, loving, accepting beings themselves. Those raised by parents who love conditionally, being warm and loving when the child behaves as desired, but withdrawing love when he or she does not, tend to learn to turn their love on and off as well.

Those who are loved unconditionally assume there is an endless supply of love available to them. Those loved conditionally come to believe that love is restricted or rationed, and develop anxiety about it. They want to hoard it, or control it, in order to alleviate their anxiety about losing it, or not getting enough. They may not give it too freely either, seeing it more as a gift or a bonus they give to those who please them. Like land in the above example, it becomes something to be possessed and traded, rather than something to be embraced, savored, celebrated and shared abundantly. Further, with its limited perspective, ego sees love as something it must get from others, rather than an endless stream at the core of one's own being into which we can tap at will.

It is here that we find the roots of jealousy, competition and control in the arena of love. Little girls, more so than boys it seems, often have difficulty with the concept of everyone playing together. You cannot be *my* friend, if you are *her* friend. If you and I are friends, then *she* can't play with us. Further, if a friend crosses a female, that may be the end of the friendship. A male is more likely to express his anger at his buddy, and then carry on as usual.

ADOLESCENT IDEAS ABOUT LOVE

As children grow into adolescents, their concept of love expands from the love they have felt for family into a new kind of love. Prior to mass media, the experience of romantic love often took one by surprise—something new stirring in the heart. There has been a loss of innocence for young people in the Western world as movies and television have distorted what should be a mature, adult kind of loving, into something that looks like more of a sport! The depth of human loving relationships cannot be adequately portrayed in the media; consequently, young people may be confused about what is real and appropriate. Disillusionment sets in because marriage requires more than a soap opera romance, a white gown and a diamond worth two months of his salary

LOVE AS NEED

Often, a relationship is judged on the basis of 'how much he/she loves me', because this feeds ego's insatiable desire for validation, acceptance, and worthiness. However, that love may be based on the partner's own need, or projections about who the other is. As time passes, the couple must deal with the complexities of life. Each may no longer be the prime focus of the other. Ego interprets this as loss of love: it is not *receiving* as much love as it needs. Love is seen as a commodity, rather than a process.

In a soulful relationship, individuals recognize ego's self-centered agenda and attempt to keep that out of their dealings with the other. It is for each individual to 'tame' his or her own ego, so it does not go about insisting the partner meet its demands. The soulful relationship is one in which each individual brings his or her own soul to the union, and the loving energies of each blend. They thus tap into the stream of loving consciousness, drawing it into their beings, at the same time as their loving energy flows out into the world.

Ego's love is too often about control, need, self-centeredness and ownership. This is true whether it is love for a partner, or a child. Ego wants the object of love to fulfill its wishes, desires and expectations: to 'be there for me'. Soulful loving allows individuals to be who they are, and supports them in expressing their individuality and uniqueness. The joy in soulful loving comes in watching the other take flight, even if that flight means the loved one goes away. A purpose has been fulfilled, and on the level of soul there is no separation.

CONDITIONAL LOVE IN MARRIAGE

I recall a couple who had been married almost fifteen years. Their plan had been to start a family, with the wife staying home to raise the children, while the husband built his business. They had three children, and indeed, the wife was very involved in nurturing them, and also in organizing and implementing their many activities. The husband worked hard at his business, and although suffering from stress, he was financially successful. Once the children were all in school, the wife, who had been involved in dancing as a young adult, decided to become involved in it again. She joined a dance troupe, and went to practice a couple of times a week. As the time approached for a major performance, rehearsals increased, so that she was out more often, and arriving home later. She felt herself coming alive again, and knew she wanted dancing to be part of her life as long as possible. She also enjoyed the social connection with others who also loved dance.

In the weeks prior to the performance, she did let the housework slide, and her husband found himself preparing most of the meals. Anger and resentment began to build. He felt abandoned and betrayed: his interpretation was that she was breaking her original agreement to be a stay-at-home Mom. She was resentful that after spending more than ten years focused only on home and family, he would not support her in doing something she loved.

For a long time, neither was able to appreciate the point of view of the other. His ego felt threatened: she was not being who he wanted her to be. He felt that she did not love him or care about the family. Love, for his ego, meant her living up to the image of wife and mother he had in his mind. If she really loved him, she would stop this nonsense completely, stay at home, clean the house and have supper ready.

Her ego felt threatened as well. It knew what it wanted, and expected full and complete support. Love, for her ego, meant the husband would do double-duty as long as necessary, would be tolerant when she came home late after rehearsals or post-performance parties.

His ego led him to respond like an authoritarian father, laying out the rules in no uncertain terms. He let her know that the survival of their marriage depended on her making 'better' choices.

Her ego led her to respond like a rebellious teenager. She would do what she wanted, and would make him wrong for expressing his feelings, accusing him of trying to control her. Their egos had them locked into a power struggle, from which neither knew how to escape. Although they loved one another, they talked of separating so she could pursue her dream, and he could find someone who would be content to fill the role he envisioned for a wife.

If the couple shifted to a soul-based perspective, things could be quite different. He would recognize that her dancing was her passion—a creative expression of her spirit. He might look for ways to arrange their lives to accommodate some of what she was needing. She would realize that he was fearful of losing her to the world of dance, and might reassure him of her love and commitment to him and the family. Together they might arrange for extra household help to relieve him of some of the burden when she was busy, and make a point of scheduling specific family activities and couple-time, so everyone could stay connected.

Soul-based love is accommodating, understanding, flexible, and compassionate. Its desire is as much for the comfort and happiness of the loved one as for its own joy. Ego does not give up control easily, and often does not even realize there *are* other choices.

CONTROLLING LOVE

I once worked with a young woman who, despite being intelligent and motivated to make a success of her life, sabotaged herself at every turn. It was a struggle to keep organized and focused, and the closer she got to achieving a goal, the more anxious she became—and the more likely she was to mess up. She was immobilized by fear: she did not believe in herself, and was sure she would fail at anything she tried.

It was puzzling to watch her as she would start out with good intentions, and then it was as though an invisible shield surrounded her, preventing her from completing what she set out to do. Puzzling, that is, until I discovered a little more about the dynamics in her family. As she was growing up, her parents did everything for her. She was not allowed to take responsibility for things herself. For her parents, loving a child meant doing everything for that child. In their minds, if the child needed them, then they felt loved. Consequently, as the child began to strive for independence, there was a subtle sense of guilt projected by the parents. As the young woman became an adult, her parents still needed her to need them. If she wanted to do things herself, or turned down their offers of help, they acted hurt and depressed.

It was unthinkable for her even to discuss these behaviors with them, as she felt they would be crushed. What was really going on for this client was not a fear of failure, but rather a *fear of success.* Success would mean growing up, moving on, and not needing her parents. Knowing how much they had invested emotionally in keeping her weak and dependent, she would always crash just as she began to gain strength. This kind of love is typical of ego's grasping and holding. The parent's egos sucked the life force out of the daughter, to fulfill their own needs. The daughter's ego, unable to tolerate the rejection and guilt that success would trigger, unconsciously *colluded* with the egos of her parents, to maintain the status quo.

SOULFUL LOVING

Soulful loving is different. It is expansive and allowing. It recognizes that each individual has his or her own journey, and no one else is responsible for fulfilling our emotional needs. We cannot latch onto another person, be it a child, friend or partner, and expect their energy to fill a void within us, or lift us to a higher level. Loved ones bless us by *sharing* our lives, but we must not try to make them *be* our lives.

Love is a process that brings joy as it flows around us and through us. Like a butterfly, it delights and surprises us, warming our hearts as it flutters through our lives. Its beauty is in its freedom, and we can no more clutch and hold it than we can confine the captured butterfly to a jar. We can try, but it is just not the same.

EXERCISES

1) Think of two or three people you love.
2) List three emotional needs you expect each person to fulfill.
3) Think of conflicts or differences you have with each person. How many of those are associated with their failure to fulfill the expectations listed above?
4) How would things be different if you did not hold those expectations?
5) Think of those who love you.
6) List any emotional needs you think they expect you to fulfill.
7) Are you uncomfortable with any of those expectations?
8) How would things be different if they did not hold those expectations of you?

Chapter 7

LOVE IN FAMILIES

PARENTS AND CHILDREN

Our experiences with love and pain in our family of origin powerfully impact all of our adult relationships. The family is where we have our first experiences with love, acceptance, rejection, abandonment, and even indifference. We may well spend the rest of our lives playing out some of the dynamics of our family of origin, or reacting to others on the basis of our experiences there. The level of trust that we can hold is established as a result of our early years. Our level of openness is also determined then. If we feel safe and cared for, we learn to express our emotions. If not, we learn to suppress and hide them.

 We come into the world as pure souls, pure potential. Ideally, if the world were a Garden of Eden, all of our needs would be met, we would be surrounded by love, and could explore to our heart's content. We would slowly, easily, and naturally blossom into the full manifestation of our unique spirit. Instead, we are shaped and molded by the egos of all who surround us.

My Mother was not happy upon discovering she was pregnant with me. When I was born, both parents were disappointed I was not a boy. When I came home from the hospital, my two-year old sister reached into the bassinet and slapped my face! This was no Garden of Eden, and I was a disappointment, not a blessing. Even a loving welcome can be dominated by ego. The parents who delight at the birth of their son, visualizing a future hockey player or doctor, are already beginning to shape this new soul to an image satisfying to *their* egos. If they picture frilly dresses and pretty bows for their daughter, her childhood may be marked by power struggles over what she chooses to wear.

In Western culture, the psyche has generally been dominated by ego. It takes a parent who is connected to, and reverent of his or her own soul, to raise a child soulfully. Since that has not been the norm, most of us are the product of ego influences. For generations, children have been treated as 'possessions'. Child-rearing has been a process of shaping children according to the belief systems of the parents. This is not a bad thing. It was parents doing what they believed was right, and best for all. Good parenting meant training the child to be acceptable and functional in society.

There was no room in this system, however, for the soul of the child. Not knowing what to do with it, adults simply left it out of the equation. Is it any wonder that we have to work hard to learn how to be soulful in relationships? It is much like years ago, when parents did not want their child to be left-handed. The child would pick up a spoon or crayon with the left hand, and the parents would consistently remove it and place it in the right hand. Eventually the child, born with a dominant left hand, developed right-handedness. Schooling may have been a bit of a struggle, but by adulthood, if this individual tried to use the left hand, it would feel awkward and strange, even though at one time it was the natural way. So it is with soul.

Occasionally, in the life of a child, there is an adult—relative, teacher or coach, who sees into the soul of that child. No words are spoken to that effect, but in the presence of that person, the child feels a wonderful expansiveness and acceptance. All they know at the time is they really like that person. When they get older, and begin to bring their soul forth in awareness, they remember the feeling and the person with whom they first felt it. This experience happens because the individual who sees the child's soul has no ego involvement, and consciously or not, is connecting at a soul level with the child.

For the most part, however, the child speaks in the language spoken to him or her. If adults are speaking from ego, the child responds from ego. Since most adults have been ego-based, that is the modality that is developed in children. This has had profound implications for our experience of love.

CONDITIONAL LOVE

Recall that when life is interpreted from the perspective of ego, it becomes characterized by conditional love. When adult egos like what the child does, positive judgement is communicated with a sense of accomplishment, reward, satisfaction, and pride. If adult egos do not like what the child does, the judgement is negative, communicated with a sense of disappointment, dissatisfaction, shame, or sorrow. If this is not enough to cause the child to align more with external expectations, the adult may create polarity, becoming adversarial, confrontational, resentful, blaming, and punishing.

Most children, being dependent on parents or caregivers, find polarity too threatening, and consequently, like flowers turning to the light, they begin to shape themselves into an acceptable form. At an early age they learn that to be loved, one must be acceptable. To be acceptable, one must conform. To conform, one must give up big parts of the self. These are given up willingly, and early enough in life that they are forgotten. This works well for all. Parents and teachers pride themselves in having done a good job. Things go along smoothly until some of the sleeping souls get restless. This often happens in adolescence.

The 'psychic anesthetic' administered in childhood begins to wear off, for some, in adolescence. There is a burning desire to 'be myself'. Having had few, if any models of unique soulful expression, there is confusion in the adolescent consciousness. Something unique is yearning to be expressed, but the 'what' and 'how' are not clear. Like Lorenz's ducks, who bonded with a dog in the psychology experiment because that was what was there when they hatched, adolescents, 'bond' with their peers and their music. A new energy is awakening in them, and they reach for something that takes them beyond the consciousness experienced in their families. Much as 'thirty-somethings' think they will never give up their youthful tastes in music, by the time their children are teenagers, there is a new generation of music to which they cannot listen, much less relate. Music unites the younger generation, and differentiates them from the previous one.

The urge to be themselves drives teens to dress differently, wear their hair differently, talk differently, and to pierce and tattoo their bodies. They often become very creative, expressing themselves in music, art or writing. Their souls are desperately trying to find expression. Unfortunately, like the left-handed child, the message they get from adult egos is that they are doing it wrong, it is just a stage, and we hope they will grow out of it soon. Those who cannot squeeze themselves back into the bottle of conformity, move farther out into the fringes of society. The others, in time, give up this wild and carefree period of free expression, herding themselves back into the pack.

Things may then tick along nicely for another twenty years, when a mid-life crisis hits, and is recognized as perhaps a last chance to honor the soul's journey, sidetracked almost from the moment of birth. Soul is like a germinating seed pushing its way up through the dark soil of ego consciousness. There is an undeniable urging, propensity, or inclination to move towards the light.

Many conditions can stunt or block the growth of a plant, or the growth of a soul. Some plants never see the light of day, and sadly, some souls remain buried for a lifetime. Given the right conditions, blossoming comes naturally. Families are the first gardens of the soul. The most vital nutrients for an emerging soul are unconditional love and acceptance. Sadly, few get a consistent supply of these nutrients; so, soul remains encased in the seed jacket of ego, unable to freely burst forth.

UNCONDITIONAL LOVE

Those throughout history who have transformed the world in positive ways have been ones who were unafraid to speak their truth, and to live their lives according to that truth. They did this even if they were persecuted or crucified. Righting wrongs, or correcting injustices was more important to them than conforming to the norms of their times. It is such individuals who have set the standards for the evolution of human consciousness.

When children are loved conditionally, they learn to conform to the expectations of others. With this, they learn to watch others, to see how their words or behaviors are being received. There is a fear of displeasing others, or being rejected. This is the development of *self*-consciousness. As their attention becomes increasingly focused on what others think of them, they begin to shape themselves to increase the likelihood of positive responses. It becomes safer to repeat behaviors and ideas which are known to be accepted, than to risk a more individualistic expression, and possible rejection or ridicule. Perhaps that is why individuals like Jesus, Gandhi, or Martin Luther King are so rare. They were able to stand apart from the tribe and follow their inner knowing.

Loving conditionally literally trains children to please others rather than honoring themselves. For many, being good parents means raising children who are little models of themselves. Evolutionary growth is stunted. Each generation, being a later model, is more evolved than the one before. However, if they are not given the opportunity and encouragement to express what is in their souls, that evolutionary potential is lost.

Loving unconditionally does not mean children are given free rein to do whatever they please. It does mean that the individuality of each being is honored, and children are encouraged to express their own thoughts and views. Further, it means they are not judged for how they think, even if their thoughts run opposite to ours. We can teach them to love and honor their perspectives by valuing them ourselves. We can seek their opinions almost as soon as they can talk. We can listen, and listen, and listen. Ask a five year old intriguing questions, and watch how empowered they become as they formulate creative answers. I used to ask my children things like where they were before they were born, and why we had only one moon. Prior to going to school, children will not hesitate to explain their theories in great detail. Once they have learned the concept of right and wrong answers, they might not answer such questions at all, or else they will simply tell you they do not know.

Unconditional loving means helping children to understand they are unique and special beings who *belong* in this world. Teaching them that each and every one of us is needed here, and that we are each here to make our own special contribution, whatever that may be, allows them to value and pursue their individuality. Conditional loving creates a contraction of energy in both parent and child. Unconditional loving is expansive, and both parent and child feel uplifted when such energy is exchanged.

Let us look now at some practical situations that arise for parents, illustrating the process and consequences of ego-based and soul-based parenting.

THE REPORT CARD

Recall that ego interpretation of life events is characterized by judgement, which may be negative or positive. Negative judgements can also lead to polarity. At the ego-based end of the continuum of consciousness, the issue of school grades becomes tied in with the status or value of the child. High marks bring rewards, parents are pleased and proud, and the child feels good. The child feels good because there is an 'A' on the report card, not because of what he or she has learned. Marks are an example of extrinsic reward or motivation. The letter grade really has no connection whatever with the content of what was taught or learned.

Low marks, on the other hand, are met with disappointment, dissatisfaction and even shame. A child may be achieving to the best of his ability, but feels mediocre because his marks are mediocre. A child may be intelligent and knowledgeable, but get a failing grade because she did not do the work. This child may feel stupid, and consider herself a failure. If a child consistently gets low marks, the situation may evolve into polarity, where there is a power struggle between the student and parents. This process may be characterized by confrontation, blame, resentment, and punishment.

Interestingly, even the student who gets high marks can suffer from low self-esteem. Once she experiences the positive regard that comes with good performance, she may then live with the fear of losing that regard. Honor students often have tremendous anxiety about maintaining their standing, and can become quite depressed if their marks drop, even if they are still in the honors range. Marks, high or low, are a form of judgement. Learning in the broadest sense may be compromised, as teachers teach to the portion of knowledge tested, and students study what they think will be on the test. At higher levels, projects may be designed, and papers written with the teacher's or professor's biases in mind, in hopes of a higher mark.

Learning, from a soulful perspective, would be quite different. The child's imagination and curiosity would be the starting point. Learning would be an adventure, valued for its own sake. Children would learn to use their minds to facilitate the expression of their unique essence. Since their ideas would be valued, they would be motivated to develop and express more of them. Basic skills would be the 'tools' they develop along the way to support their creative expression. The focus would be on what they produced with these tools, not on the tools themselves. Thinking and expression in various forms would be welcomed, supported and encouraged, not graded.

Schools do not teach like that, so even the soulful parent must deal with the report card. A positive report card is an occasion for the parent to share in the child's sense of accomplishment, but the focus would be on how much was learned, or how much effort was put forth, rather than on the mark itself. Ideally, the child enjoyed the learning, and in the process got a good mark. The learning is the goal—not the mark.

A report card with low marks is received by the soulful parents non-judgmentally. There is an *understanding* that there were some problems with that subject. The parent responds *compassionately,* offering encouragement and help. *Trust* is expressed that all can work together to ensure more learning. *Love* and *acceptance* of the child are demonstrated, so he knows low marks do not affect his parent's regard for him. For the soulful parent, marks are an indicator of school performance, not a measure of the worth, or even the intelligence of the child. This approach allows the child to keep believing in himself, while continuing to work towards surmounting difficulties, rather than giving up and seeing himself as incapable of learning. It also builds a sense of security in the child, for he knows that he is loved and loveable, independently of his performance.

MISBEHAVIOR

Every child will misbehave at some point. A toddler's natural instinct is to explore. Given the opportunity, a toddler will get into anything and everything. Because parents are concerned with safety, they must teach the child the meaning of the word 'no'. The expectation is once the child understands 'no' means Mommy and Daddy do not want you to touch that, then the child should obey that command. What we are asking is that the child modify his natural curiosity and biological instincts upon hearing the command. This is a conditioned response. Compliance brings smiles, warmth and loving responses. Defiance brings stern faces, louder voices, coolness, and sometimes angry responses. It may also bring banishment (into your room you go). Because compliance is equated with 'goodness,' and defiance with 'badness', it is a short step to labeling children as good or bad depending on how obedient they are.

You can see how, right from the beginning, ego interpretation shapes the world of the child. If a positive judgement is made of the child's behavior, she is rewarded, and encouraged to feel proud of herself. If a negative judgement is made, then the child is responded to with disappointment, is blamed or punished, and is encouraged to feel ashamed of herself.

Of course it is possible to train children to behave appropriately, safely, and cooperatively, without ever bringing in judgement. The toddler can be simply moved away and distracted from inappropriate objects or places. Parenting from a soulful perspective means *understanding* how curious the child is, and how desirable objects may seem. It means having *compassion* for the child's desires and frustrations, and *acceptance* of behaviors that are typical for the age or stage of the child.

This does not mean that soulful parents do not have struggles, or never send a child to his room. The difference is the child is not sent to his room as punishment. He is sent there to cool down, to think about things, to make a wise choice, or to have a good cry. As he is carried off to his room, the parent may hug him, and tell him he is loved, even if he is in the midst of a tantrum. He is encouraged to re-join the family as soon as he is feeling more co-operative. Grudges are not held, nor are records kept of misbehavior. A child's behavior is not compared with that of a sibling, nor is the child made to feel guilty.

COMMON SENSE

Common sense is good judgement based on experience. Children are not born with it, but, like the rest of us, they acquire it through trial and error. Children may make mistakes that, to adults, seem obviously avoidable. Soulful parenting does not judge children for errors, which are part of the learning process. Many children have had the experience of taking something from a store, because they wanted it badly, and it was in easy reach. Parents become alarmed, because this is stealing, and they do not want their child becoming a thief. In the process however, they make their child *feel* like a thief. Ego judges quickly, and, coming from fear, reacts without thinking. Soul-based parenting recognizes the out-of-control ego desire that prompted the impulsive act. There is compassion for the hard learning the child has drawn to herself, and acceptance of the healing process. The parent ensures that the child returns to the store, admitting to the deed and making restitution. This is sufficient consequence, and the lesson is generally learned.

The child is lovingly supported throughout, although the *behavior* is clearly not accepted. This leaves the integrity of the child intact, and she is no doubt eager to retain it. This contrasts sharply with the ego-based response that expresses extreme disappointment and shame, implying the child has no integrity and cannot be trusted. If the child comes to believe this, a negative self-fulfilling prophecy is initiated. Thinking of herself as a bad person, she may repeat the misbehavior and indeed become what the parents most feared. The soulful response, on the other hand, validates the child's integrity, regarding the misbehavior as a lapse or anomaly. This generates a positive self-fulfilling prophecy. Feeling that she is a person of integrity, her future behaviors will be in alignment with that belief.

TEENAGERS

Teenagers have been the most maligned segment of Western culture. If comments frequently made about teenagers were made about any other group within our society, they would be considered discriminatory and politically incorrect in the extreme. Teens have been ridiculed for the way they dress, how they wear their hair, the music they listen to, the priorities they set, the friends they choose, what they eat, and how they think. Because adolescence creates big challenges for parents and educators, and the model of the child conforming to the expectations of adults begins to break down, adolescents are seen as the weak link in the system.

It is the system, however, which was flawed from the start. Since most parenting, until recently, has been done from an ego-based perspective, and since the parent's ego, for the first few years at least, is stronger than the child's, much of the parenting process has been about having the child conform. The parent's ego felt best when the child not only behaved, but also thought the same way as the parents. It was not only behavior that was shaped, but thinking as well. Consequently, if a parent believed aggression should be met with aggression, the child was taught to fight back. If he did not, he was a sissy. If a parent believed physical force should not be used, the aggressive child was considered a bully. The child whose thoughts and behaviors did not align with his parent's was judged as wrong. The young child never knew it was a matter of perspective.

The system was flawed, because it made no allowance for the day when the child ceased to blindly accept parental views. It had no built-in program that could adapt to the child's realization that right and wrong, good and bad, were sometimes a matter of perspective. Rather than fixing the system, however, all efforts went into fixing the child.

When two opposing forces meet, a clash is inevitable. The child's budding individuality threatens the parent's control. Ego's answer to this is to exert more control. At a time when the biological imperative demands that children individuate and begin to establish identities separate from those of their parents, the ego-based parent tightens his or her grip. Frustrated when even redoubled efforts do not work, the parent may resort to intimidation, blame, criticism, judgement, rejection, and punishment. Naturally these reactions hurt, and naturally, the teen reacts with anger and rebellion. The system cannot accommodate their changing needs. The adults, not knowing how to handle this, resort to more primitive means of control, which trigger more primitive responses in their adolescent. Since ego's way is to blame, and since the adults still have more power, the problem is defined as teen rebelliousness. A self-fulfilling cycle is perpetuated as parents brace themselves for the 'teen years', anticipating problems, and gearing themselves up for squelching any signs of oppositional behavior, the earlier the better. Battle lines are drawn, but it does not have to be that way.

Let's look at parenting teenagers from a soulful perspective. Beginning at birth, soulful parents realize they do not own this child. They recognize that as the child grows, he may be nothing like his parents. Their goal is to provide a safe and loving environment in which the child can learn about himself and the world. They help him to see consequences of various behaviors, and to understand he is creating the person he is, and the life he will have. Soulful parenting honors the essence of his soul, providing gentle guidance, and sufficient information for the child to develop his own capacities for discernment and wisdom. Because differences are handled in a mutually respectful manner, the child remains free, as he grows, to express his thoughts and views. Because he is not judged for being different, or made to feel guilty for questioning his parents, he is open to much more learning.

Soulful parenting does not guarantee there will not be conflict. It does mean the parents take responsibility for restraining their own reactions, as hurtful words said in anger to a child may remain etched in consciousness forever. The experi-

Love and Families

ence of adolescence in any home may be respectfully co-created between parent and child. Beginning when a child is eleven or twelve, parents can begin talking with the child about changes that will come, and developing a plan for handling differences. If we talk with children before the hormones are raging, before they become immersed in a 'parents as bad guys' mentality, we can consciously co-create with them the experience we will have during the adolescent years.

We can explain that within the years from thirteen to eighteen, they will evolve from child to adult, and it is as difficult for parents to make that transition as it is for teens. They need to understand our need to control comes out of our fear and protectiveness, and is ultimately grounded in love. They will want increasing levels of freedom, and it is natural for parents to resist that. Consequently there will be times when agreement cannot be reached, and in those cases the parent has the deciding vote. However, adolescents need to be reassured that as we become confident in the level of wisdom and responsibility they demonstrate, we will be loosening our grip. We can ask for their support and understanding during this process, and commit to being as supportive and understanding as we can be as well. It is important also to tell them no matter what the differences or conflicts parents and children go through during this time, it is a transitional period, and we hold the goal of traversing it safely, coming out with an intact, loving relationship at the other end. Adolescence is only five years; we are parents and children for a lifetime.

A TWIST IN THE PLOT

The purpose of our time here on Earth is to evolve from ego-based humans, to soul-based beings. It does not happen in a vacuum. As discussed in the last chapter, it is our relationships with others that serve as catalysts for our growth. Our children are our greatest teachers. They will challenge the efforts of our egos to control them. They may do this through quiet resistance, or open rebellion: they give immediate feedback as to whether what we are doing is working. If we are respectful of their souls, giving them some say in their lives, they respond, for the most part, with affection and respect. If we ignore that aspect of their beings which belongs only to them, they feel misunderstood, or even violated. They respond to these feelings by distancing, polarizing, or becoming defiant or rebellious. In extreme cases they become hostile, directing anger outwardly towards others. They may also direct this anger inwards towards themselves, becoming self-destructive, self-mutilating or suicidal.

If children were like plants, we could simply provide the proper nutrients, and they could grow into healthy, balanced adults. Some parents truly are doing their best when they do all the things they believe will make their children successful adults. Generally however, it is *their own* image of a healthy, successful adult they are aiming for. If we program children to respond to external approval, then if they cannot get this approval because they do not buy into the vision parents have for them, they will get it from peers. If we teach them to develop and trust their own wisdom, to think their own thoughts, they cannot be so easily influenced.

What children teach us, if we are open to the learning, is the art of surrender. Surrender does not mean giving up and allowing them to do as they please. It means surrendering our power over them, and working *with* them. It means allowing them to fully express their views and opinions, without shutting them down. If we value their opinions from the time they are small, they will *want* to talk with us. If we ask for their help in assisting us to really understand their point of view, they will take the risk of showing us their true selves.

Children also teach us by being mirrors. Generally, the things that irritate parents most about their children are aspects of their personalities that are just like the parent's. We may try to change in them what we first need to change in ourselves. Children also trigger our anger, frustration, impatience, and tendency to judge. In other words, they show us all the places where ego still has a hold on us. It is easy to blame a child's behavior for our reactions, but that is the rationalization of our ego. If parents lose their tempers, hit their children, or yell and scream, then the children will lose their tempers, hit others, or yell and scream. If parents use ridicule, sarcasm, or put-downs, the children will use ridicule, sarcasm, and put-downs. Rude, disrespectful, and inappropriate behaviors in children reflect what they have learned. Even if they pick up such behaviors outside the home, a gentle response from parents is the best way to discourage them.

The day will come when our children will question our values, beliefs and behaviors. Young people are insightful, and can see discrepancies or incongruities a mile away. The ego-based parent may react with defensiveness, anger or even hurt. The child then learns either that speaking his truth is too risky, or inappropriate. He has no model for responding graciously to an honest challenge. Developing the ability to have honest, intimate communication is compromised. That ability is critical for healthy adult relationships. If we send children off into adulthood with this handicap, history simply repeats itself, and the evolutionary progression is halted. They struggle in their intimate relationships, and raise children reactively from ego, rather than proactively from soul. The system is still not healed, and it is no surprise that teenagers continue to have the reputation for always being so 'difficult'.

EVOLUTIONARY RESPONSIBILITY

Animals do not worry about evolution. Their focus is on survival, so they follow their biological instincts. As humans, we are beginning to recognize the incredible potential we have to influence the evolution of our species. By bringing consciousness to our actions and interactions, we influence the collective consciousness that shapes destinies of individuals, the human family and the planet itself. I cannot imagine a more profound task than being psychological or spiritual midwives to the emerging souls of our children. We can allow our souls to sleep through this lifetime, leaving our unconscious egos to replicate that unconsciousness in our children, or we can recognize we have the power to assist in the creation of exciting evolutionary shifts. The choice is ours.

EXERCISES

1) Think of messages your parents gave you as a child.
2) How did you feel when you heard those messages?
3) Give examples of messages you received expressing conditional love.
4) Give examples of messages you received expressing unconditional love.
5) How have those messages affected your self-concept as an adult?
6) Think of messages you give to your children.
7) List the ones expressing conditional love.
8) List the ones expressing unconditional love.
9) Imagine you are the soul of each one of your children. Write a letter to yourself in which each soul asks what it needs most from you in order to blossom.

10) List the changes you would like to make in order to respond more soulfully to your children.

ADULT FAMILIES

Often there are as many challenges in dealing with adult families, as there are between parents and growing children. The more ego-based our relationships have been with other family members, the more struggle we are likely to encounter in relationship with them. In some cases, certain family dynamics are still functioning twenty, thirty, or fifty years after they were set in motion initially. It is difficult for ego to release its beliefs about family members, for it has had a lifetime of conditioning. Ego also has selective perception. It sees what it wants to see. If you had a sister who was bossy and controlling when you were a child, you may still see her that way, although she may have changed substantially. Her behaviors may trigger feelings you had about her years ago, so you may find yourself pulling away from her. Her friends and colleagues, on the other hand, may see her as a strong leader, and admire her outspokenness. They may accept her unconditionally, while you are still judging her, based on your past experiences with her.

If you always felt your parents liked your brother best, ego may feel resentful of any of his adult achievements, particularly when your parents brag about him. If he were a friend, and not your brother, you likely would celebrate his achievements.

Ego's perceptions are naturally biased, because ego evaluates people and situations in relation to itself, rather than objectively. Therefore, it makes a difference if you were the oldest, the youngest or a middle child. For most of his life, a younger child may resent the fact that an older sibling always has more privileges, and gets to do things first. And older sibling may feel the youngest gets more attention, gets away with more, and has fewer demands made upon him. Meanwhile the middle child resents both due to all of the above. An older child may be expected to take care of younger ones, or be the one blamed when things go wrong. The oldest child's share of parental attention is diminished with each subsequent child, while the youngest never experiences being the sole recipient of the combined parental affections of the mother and father.

In the childhood years, ego's identity is largely defined by one's place in the family. You are a son or a daughter, a brother or a sister, a niece or a nephew, a grandson or granddaughter. Depending on how others respond to you, you are a good child or a bad child, loved or unlovable, easy or difficult, welcomed or unwelcome.

It is in these relationships where we learn to reach out or pull back, to share or to hoard, to make peace or make war, and even to love ourselves or hate ourselves. The more ego-based our interactions with these significant others in childhood, the more ego-based we are when we reach adulthood.

If we can look back at those childhood experiences, and understand the perspectives of the others in our lives, we can begin to transcend the old reality. If we can see that our big sister was bossy because our parents made her responsible for us, and not because she was inherently mean, then we can let go of the past. We are free to see her as the adult she is now; free from the shadow of the projections we created back then. It is pretty tough to move forward if we still see her as the controlling tyrant she was when she was nine years old.

PARENTS

Regardless of how old we are, how successful we have been, or how evolved we are, we may still find ourselves dancing to the beat of our parent's drum. If parents are coming from an ego-based perspective, they may still feel their children ought to be pleasing them. They may express the view that their children 'owe them' for the parenting they have done. The ego-based parent places many expectations upon his or her adult children, and if they are not met, such parents respond with hurt, anger or laying on guilt.

I have worked with clients who, although well into middle age, continued to be intimidated and controlled by a parent. If you spend the first eighteen years of life afraid of your father, or tiptoeing around so as not to make him angry, it is difficult to suddenly reclaim your power. In fact, you may go through life giving up your power to anyone who is angry or controlling. If your mother was a perfectionist, you may still find yourself frantically cleaning the house when she is on her way to visit, or worrying about appearances when *anyone* comes over.

Some adult children, though physically having left home, have never left emotionally. Some parents never allow their children to move on and live their own lives. We say these families are *enmeshed*, and generally there are problems maintaining healthy boundaries. In effect, though living apart, the original family structure and dynamics are very much present.

A soul-based perspective recognizes we are guardians or stewards of our children, protecting and nurturing them so that their souls may blossom forth. It recognizes that they have their own lives, thoughts and dreams. Loving them unconditionally means we do not take care of them with the expectation that they will someday repay the favor. We do not parent them with the expectation that they will be like us, or be what *we* want them to be. Unconditionally loving our children means setting them free to be whomever they choose to be.

A soul-based relationship between parents and their adult children is one in which, as the children reach adulthood, the relationship becomes one of equals. Although they are still *our* children, they are *not* children. Much as we might, at times, want to parent them, we treat them with the same respect we would accord any other adults in our lives. Just because we raised them as children, it does not give us the right to criticize them when they are adults (unless they are hurting someone or breaking the law, in which case they clearly still need parenting). Soulful adult family relationships are characterized by respect, understanding, compassion and acceptance.

ABUSIVE PARENTS

How does one, from a soulful-perspective, deal with the issue of childhood abuse in relation to parents? This is a very complex and often confusing question. The ego of the parent has orchestrated abusive behaviors towards a child. The ego of the child has suffered the pain, fear, and humiliation of that abuse. The damage has undoubtedly distorted the feelings and perceptions of the child, and which continues to impact adult life until that damage has been healed.

If parents are still abusive or dysfunctional, the only healthy choice may be to distance from them. It is not so easy to distance from the inner pain, though. Even when parents have mellowed into caring, supportive grandparents, it can be difficult to discuss childhood pain with them. It can be devastating if they deny our pain, but on the other hand, adult children often worry about causing older parents to feel pain and guilt in their senior years. What is needed is a way to lift the recollection of our history out of the scrapbook of ego, with all of its hurts, anger, disappointment, resentment, and feelings of victimization, and place it into the context of a soul's journey. Consider the following metaphorical fable:

Aeons ago, there was a faraway planet where souls

rested between incarnations. It was a very pleasant space, where the energy of souls blended into a loving resonance. If desired, a soul could remain there throughout eternity. Occasionally, a special call went out for volunteers.

On Planet Earth, there was an evolutionary process that was unfolding. Souls were incarnating into human beings, and these beings reproduced themselves in a genetic succession. Ideally, each generation was more highly evolved than the ones before. In some instances the evolutionary process became blocked, and consequently some Earth 'families' were locked into a destructive pattern. It appeared almost like a kind of spiritual mutation, which resulted in negative human qualities reappearing generation after generation.

The call that went out was for souls who would volunteer to be born into these troubled family systems, so that they could shift the evolutionary pattern. Many very evolved souls stepped forward immediately. They were cautioned that the assignment would be extremely difficult. They would have complete amnesia about the peaceful paradise, which now surrounded them. They would be born as an innocent child into one of these troubled family systems, and would have to suffer the pain of the negative, even destructive patterns. They might also have to endure a childhood with little, if any love. In many cases, they would feel rejected and abandoned. For most of their lives, they may feel somehow that they just do not 'belong' on Earth. Their pain would be so deep, so profound as to be almost unbearable. The evolved souls accepted the challenge, even knowing this, for they knew that they had the strength to endure.

They did not know beforehand that the experience of their childhood pain would be so deeply etched upon their consciousness, that as they grew they would easily identify with the pain of others. When they had children of their own, their deepest commitment would be to do things differently than the generations before them. A consciousness would be awakened within, which allowed them to see the mistakes of the past, and how souls had been dishonored through the generations.

They would become the architects of a new way of being. They would model this way for their own children, and for all who knew them. Still, it would not be easy. They would always struggle a little because of the profound contrast between their inner soul essence, and their beliefs about themselves on the level of ego, where most of their Earth learning transpired. However, their presence on the Earth would be profound, because their children, and their children's children would have a legacy of love and wisdom to carry into their futures. One river of negativity and darkness would have been rerouted.

It does not matter if the fable is true or not. What matters is whether we are able to shift out of the ego perspective of our past. If we are not blindly repeating the patterns of our parents, it means we are evolving. If we raise our children in ways that honor their souls, then we are instrumental in creating a shift at that intersection between all that came before in our families, and all that will come after.

ADULT SIBLINGS

Sibling relationships amongst adults can be the most rewarding, supportive relationships in our lives, or the most painful.

That is because the roots of our feelings about sisters and brothers go very deep. If there were no strong connections, positive or negative, in childhood, then the adult relationships may be low-key as well, perhaps even bordering on indifference. This sometimes happens when there is a large age spread between siblings, with one leaving home while another is still very young.

The quality of sibling relationships may be strongly determined by parenting practices, and the way matters of fairness and discipline were handled. If one sibling was always blamed for problems, and the other given the benefit of the doubt, there will be resentment. If a parent favors one child, even if he or she tries to hide that, children can tune in to that feeling, and begin to hate the favored sibling. This also can create a lifetime of competition between siblings. If the focus in parenting was on loving and honoring family members despite differences, and teaching healthy ways for children to resolve their conflicts, siblings will likely have healthy adult relationships.

Recall that ego is centered on its own experiences, and its own *perception* of those experiences. The child's ego, particularly, is unable to see the bigger picture, and consequently the memory of that ego may be very one-sided. Even if the memory of the experiences is accurate, the child's ego cannot fully understand the context that was operating at the time.

One may remember an older sibling being bossy and controlling, and carry years of resentment over it. What may not be known is the punishment the older one received each time the younger ones misbehaved. Older siblings are often inappropriately placed in the role of surrogate parents. The ego of the inner child may carry the judgements formed in childhood forward into adult life. Consequently, a sibling may still be viewed as the bossy or controlling one, the spoiled baby of the family, or the favored child even though the childhood years are long past.

Ego reactions impact on the current relationship in the following ways. One sibling gets a promotion, and an older sibling may see this as just one more instance of the younger one being spoiled and getting whatever she wants. A younger sibling may view the situation as one more example in a long history of the older one getting everything.

Parents may find themselves, even with their grown children, having to go to great lengths to keep things equal, be it gifts to the grandchildren or time spent with each child, for fear that a child will perceive favoritism. One of the biggest impediments to healthy relationships in adult families is the playing out of the old family dynamics. Often this process keeps the participants stuck in ego perceptions and reactions. Because the reactions are so long standing, it is easy to believe ego's perceptions reflect reality. This in turn makes it exceedingly difficult to realize that we do have a choice in how we perceive our experiences in family, and the family members themselves. This shift can only occur when we make a conscious choice to consider a soulful perspective.

SOUL SIBLINGS

Our siblings are those with whom, and in relation to whom, we developed our ego consciousness. Those fortunate to have parents with a loving, soulful perspective may have been helped to see and value the soul behind the ego actions and reactions. Such parents consistently remind their children that although a sibling's behavior may have been inappropriate, the sibling is not a bad person. Again and again, these children are taught to forgive, to move past judgement and polarity, and to move back into loving, or at least accepting, space. They do not form a toxic backlog of resentment and hurt feelings, which, like radioactive waste, continues to seep up and contaminate the environment for years or generations. I know of a family within which the grandmother stopped speaking to her sister when they were in their forties, and maintained the silence for the rest of their lives. Of the grandmother's children, there were some who spent most of their adult lives estranged from one another. And within the families of her children's children, a pattern of estrangement from siblings continued. What this meant also is that there were cousins who never met each other—never met their aunts and uncles. Inter- and intra-generational pathways were permanently blocked because of ego interpretations and reactions. Patterns of competition, jealousy, rivalry and hurt sabotaged adult relationships, because no one knew they could choose to transcend them.

If we can step back for a moment, we can view difficult sibling relationships from another perspective. These may be the relationships from which we have most to learn. We can change our friends, or leave a relationship and then the relationship is over. A relationship with a sibling is never really over. A sister is always a sister, and a brother a brother, even if we have removed them from our lives.

What is significant and most important about these relationships is not what the sibling has done wrong, not what is dysfunctional about him or her, but rather *what we think and do about it.* That is where our learning is. If a sibling acts without integrity, does that draw us out of our own integrity? If we felt inferior to a sister or brother as a child, have we chosen to go through life judging ourselves as inferior? If a sibling rejects us, do we become hostile and bitter, or do our best to understand the pain leading to that choice? Can we live and let live? Can we allow siblings to grow up into whomever they choose, without expectations and obligations about what or who they should be in our lives? Can we see them as adults with their own minds, their own meanings, and their own journey, of which we shared only a portion? Can we understand we did not choose them, or they us, but that they provide an exceptional opportunity to practice unconditional love, acceptance, non-judgment, and compassion? Can we see that even if the learning we have with them is to set boundaries or walk away, this can still be done with nonjudgmental compassion, and we can still feel okay about ourselves?

If we can do these things with a sibling, the one with whom the roots of our pain may go the deepest, then we can do it with anyone. In fact, when any of our relationships become dysfunctional, we may well be reverting to reactions and behaviors we used with our brothers and sisters. If we can respond to sibling relationships regardless of their state, from a place of health within ourselves, we have taken a huge step in dealing with difficulties in *any* of our relationships.

CONCLUSION

It is much easier to get soulful with friends and lovers, than it is with family. Sometimes there is a huge resistance to soulfulness with family members because it is with them we feel most vulnerable, perhaps from a history of pain, or feeling unsafe. At other times the resistance is because a general level of comfort has been established over the years and there is a fear of stirring up the past.

It is important to remember that in the context of family, a soulful stance may be taken without involving others at all. We simply begin *being* more soulful in our thoughts, interpretations and behaviors. We do this because we are concerned about our own evolution, growth, and healing, not to elicit a 'correct' response from anyone else. Trying to heal another, or to drag them over to our healing pathway, rarely works.

It is within family that we learn about love. It may be healthy, life-enhancing learning, or unhealthy, life-sabotaging learning. If it was the former, we have a good foundation upon which to grow. If the latter, then we need to un-learn unhealthy patterns. Are we unfortunate if we have to do all this learning? I do not think so. In the process of recognizing and releasing old ways, and discovering and implementing new ones, we have a most powerful opportunity to discover our authentic selves. We often see things we never would have seen, meet people we never would have met, and have experiences we never thought we would have had, all because we ended up on a road that was not part of our carefully planned itinerary. The road to authenticity lies before us. Once again, the choice is ours.

EXERCISES

1. Think of ways in which your parents still relate to you from a place of ego.
2. Think of ways in which you relate to them from ego.
3. List some of the hurts and resentments you feel towards your parents or siblings.
4. Write a metaphorical story about the journey you have taken with your family, imagining you have come here to learn, grow, and transform old ways.
5. Consider how you would respond to family members if the metaphorical story were true, and if you were all playing significant roles in providing learning opportunities for the others.

Chapter 8

LOVE IN INTIMATE RELATIONSHIP

In the last chapter, we looked at the difference between love as expressed by ego, and love as expressed by soul. Nowhere is this difference more strikingly apparent than in the arena of intimate relationships. An intimate relationship is like a microcosm of our entire lives. It is like a stage onto which ego projects our history and beliefs relating to love, as well as all the expectations, dreams, and fantasies about what we want love to be.

Generally, I believe it is the soul that brings two people into loving relationship. In the beginning, it is so wonderful because the love is pure and unconditional. We see the best in the other person, and we give our best to the relationship. There is such joy and excitement, because two souls freely shower each other with boundless love. Hearts are open, and that loving energy of the Universe that we talked about in the last chapter flows abundantly through those hearts. When one feels this energy, there is a sense of being in love, not only with the beloved, but with life itself.

This is the experience of oneness: we feel intimately connected with all that is. We are reminded physically and emotionally of the warmth of the bonding energy we had with our mothers at birth, and perhaps cosmically of the primordial energy which first created the atoms, which now comprise our beings. This is falling in love.

COURTSHIP

Biologically we are programmed to attract, and be attracted to a mate. That is the only way the species could survive, prior to recent advances in technology. There is a biological attraction between potential mates, but, because we have an evolved left-brain hemisphere, it is often tempered with rationality and reason, though certainly not always. While some humans do mate with the first partner for whom they feel attraction, most who are reading this book would likely give some thought to characteristics that would be desirable in a mate. This sounds like a good thing, however it is often the ego which sets the criteria.

Some of those criteria are based on unconscious patterns, consequently people may truly not know what they are getting into, or why. It just seems right at the time.

Let us take a peek behind the scenes. Ego, as you recall from earlier chapters, is concerned with itself. Ego looks for fulfillment. Ego wants to be loved, respected, admired, perhaps even idolized. Most egos, though they would not admit it, would enjoy being on a pedestal, at least once in a while.

Throughout childhood and adolescence, ego never gets its fill of those qualities, if, in fact, it ever does. There is a deep hunger for complete fulfillment. Ego is like a jigsaw puzzle, with empty spaces created by missing pieces. When someone falls in love with us, ego is flooded with ecstatic feelings of warmth and acceptance, and *imagines* that with this person, the empty spaces will be filled. There is a deep sense of satisfaction and completion, with dreams of 'happily ever after' well entrenched in consciousness. Somehow this love will heal all the wounded parts; ego will have an endless supply of nourishment, and all will be well. The couple begins building a dream on this blissful foundation.

If the couple remained at this initial stage when their souls connected and the love flowed freely between them, they would remain contented. However, once ego has *imagined* fulfillment of its unhealed parts or unrealized desires, it forms the *expectation* that the partner will transform what was imagined into reality. Ego equates fulfillment of this expectation with being loved, because when bonding in love with the partner in the beginning, it *seemed* as though all needs were filled abundantly.

This creates an impossible situation, because no one else can complete our fragmented ego. The fragmentation we feel is healed only by shifting our awareness to our soul essence—that part of our being which rests in wholeness.

When my daughter was two years old, I held her in my arms one fall evening, as we watched the sun set. Where we live in Alberta, Canada, the autumn sun looks like a huge pink ball, and you can watch it sink slowly out of sight; it is breathtaking to watch it make its descent. The moment it disappeared, my older children and I stood in silence, captured by the awe of that moment. My two-year old then burst into tears; she wanted me to make the pretty ball come back. The only way she could avoid suffering that pain was to grow to a point where she could expand her awareness of the processes of nature. Then she would know that the sun would be there again the next day.

Similarly, the only way ego can avoid its suffering, is to expand its boundaries, giving way to the more expansive awareness of soul. Until ego can begin to understand the bigger picture, it continues to grasp and hold, expecting the world to conform to its expectations. That can no more happen than the earth reversing its rotation so my daughter could have the sun back. Yet, ego stubbornly insists that the loved one behave in ways that make it happy.

THE HONEYMOON IS OVER

When life with our partner does not live up to our expectations, disappointment and disillusionment set in. Remembering how good it was in the beginning, ego is intent on recapturing the bliss of the early days. Because ego felt so fulfilled then, it assumes the partner was fulfilling all its needs.

Now feeling *unfulfilled*, it assumes the partner has withdrawn love, attention, and affection, or perhaps has changed priorities. The obvious solution seems to be to do some renovations on the partner. A few changes here and there, and everything should be fine again.

What ego fails to realize is that the partner was not creating the good feelings. Ego created its own good feelings by projecting onto the partner fulfillment of all its fantasies. In the 'rush' created by falling in love, ego felt exalted, desired, complete, important, needed, and accepted. As the couple settles in to the reality of daily living, preoccupied with work, children, extended families, financial concerns and the myriad little things that demand attention, the energy they have to give one another becomes necessarily fragmented. Ego misses the intensity of the good feelings of the early days, and looks to the partner to bring it back. There are two characteristics of ego in relationship that should be noted: its focus is primarily on its own needs, and it tends to blame the partner if things are not as it wishes.

BECOMING OUR PARENTS

At the same time, as ego becomes aware that its dream of the ideal partner (leading to the ideal life) is not shaping up exactly as expected, its critical eye begins noticing other things. Thoughts and feelings are being triggered by the partner, and ego finds itself exhibiting some behavior traits more characteristic of its parent(s).

The female may be frustrated when her prince leaves his clothes lying around, and so she harps at him, finding her mother's words or tone of voice coming out of her mouth. He gets annoyed with being nagged, and puts her down, withdrawing to the garage, just as his father always did. Sometimes the behavior of an individual is a *reaction* to the way he or she was treated as a child. If a woman had a domineering father, she might respond aggressively at even a hint of authoritarianism in her mate. If a man had a mother who never had time for him as a child, he may appear controlling when he insists his partner spend more time with him.

Responding becomes more and more complicated for ego. It wants its own needs met, and then subconsciously may be fighting its parent's battles. The couple moves farther and farther away from the love that brought them together in the first place. The honeymoon is definitely over, and there may be some disillusionment with the idea of love itself.

At this point ego has a choice. It may face the fact that what it is doing is not bringing the happiness it so desires, and thus surrender to the more soulful energies of the higher self. In this case, the couple may honestly look at what has been happening, and seek assistance in getting their relationship back on track.

Alternatively, ego may stubbornly insist that the partner is the problem, and the only way to obtain the fulfillment it craves is to find a new partner. The relationship may end, or ego, moving more deeply into self-gratification, may pursue an affair outside of the union—holding on to what it sees as the best of both worlds.

In so doing, ego goes right back to the beginning, starting with projection and fantasy, seeing the new partner as 'the one' who will fulfill all that is missing. The process may repeat itself several times during a lifetime, or ego may eventually give up the search for love, settling for a 'comfortable' union that it perceives as preferable to being alone.

SOULFUL LOVING

Let us go back to the beginning now, and run through the entire relationship building process assuming a soulful, rather than ego based perspective. What would that look like? We must begin by looking at the individuals prior to their finding one another.

Imagine individuals who have evolved or healed themselves to the point where they feel good enough about themselves that they are not needing another for validation or emotional sustenance. I always say that a partner should be the icing on the cake of our lives, but never the cake itself. We must be self-sufficient, particularly emotionally, in order to contribute to a healthy union.

A soulful connection is made when ego has been tamed to the point that it is not driving the emotions. Each individual has some connection with his or her own soul, and therefore can also see into the soul of the other. There is a recognition of who the other is at the core of his or her being. Further, there is a deep respect or honoring of that essential nature. You would love that person, whether or not you were romantically connected, just because of who he or she is. There is not a sense of wanting or needing anything from that person: it is joyful simply to know them.

Once the souls have made a connection, the personalities must assess whether or not there is sufficient compatibility to share a life. If so, the relationship proceeds. It is an extension and deepening of the unconditional love and respect that was there all along.

Ego may want to jump in and begin to control things, or establish expectations, but the soulful couple, recognizing ego for what it is, will subdue those forces within themselves. If ego's energy spills over and affects the relationship, the couple works together from a soulful perspective to settle ego down. Like two parents attempting to manage children who are being unruly, they undertake this process with compassion and respect for all involved, yet remain strong enough to maintain the integrity of the relationship.

The most significant characteristic of the soulful relationship is that it is based on unconditionally loving the other, and placing as much importance on the relationship as on the individuals. The well-being of both parties is of primary importance, and both nurture the relationship as they would a delicate plant. There is a mutual 'caring for' the other, out of which love continues to blossom. Such a relationship does not have the 'me' focus of the ego based relationship: love flows in the direction of 'thee' and 'we'. In the process, the 'me' is fulfilled.

Even in soulful relationships, ego can overpower sometimes, resulting in pain and struggle. Rather than turning on one another with judgement and blame, each person looks inward, 'owning' their own 'acting out' ego. They look at what is being triggered within, and what kind of old wounds may be coming up for healing.

They see the relationship as a safe place in which such healing can occur, and in fact, see this as one of the primary functions of healthy, loving relationships. They are able to honestly and intimately share their deepest thoughts, feelings and worries. Through the process of helping one another, and preserving that safe place for doing so, the intimacy and connectedness deepens.

There is a sense of learning and growing together. Every once in a while there may be upheavals, which are then followed by a time of integration and balance. These couples are not thrown off guard when issues come up, but may welcome them as opportunities for growth and deepening awareness of themselves and the other. They practice what I call an 'ecology' of relationship. There is a recognition of toxic attitudes and behaviors, as well as the damage that an unrestrained ego can do, so they protect the 'environment' of their relationship.

It is rare however, for two very evolved and whole individuals to find each other and enter into a relationship that is completely soulful and balanced right from the start. Rather, we draw people into our lives with whom we can do the work of developing our capacity to create and sustain soulful relationships.

EGO AND SOUL IN RELATIONSHIP

When two people are drawn into relationship there is a very focused concentration of energy. We are drawn to those with whom we have something to learn, and they to us. Sometimes the learning is joyful, other times painful, but always there is learning.

In the behaviors, words, and actions of others, we see reflections of aspects of ourselves. At the level of soul consciousness, there is perfect understanding of what is occurring in terms of the learning. It is at the level of ego consciousness that struggle and difficulty arise.

As has been suggested, the direction of the evolutionary path is towards being in loving relationship with all other beings. This means developing the ability to view and relate to others from the stance of acceptance, understanding, and compassion. The farther away one is from this stance on the consciousness continuum, the greater the level of difficulty in the relationship. We may either become conflicted with, or draw away from those who do not honor our soul.

Apparent conflicts over finances, communication, or children may be a reflection of the deeper struggle to connect at the level of soul. The soul knows its path, but until there is an integration in each individual between soul and self, ego too often determines an alternate path. This may result in a pulling in opposite directions both *within* each individual as well as *between* the two of them. This manifests, in life, as struggle.

In the next section, we will look at several couples and the struggle within their relationships. We will see how ego has created problems, and how soul could avoid or resolve them.

WENDY AND DAVE

Wendy was thirty-two years old, and a sales representative for a national company. She had been married to Dave for almost ten years, and they had two young children aged four and six. Her husband was a businessman who was doing well. They had a dream of moving to a warmer climate and building their dream home. Dave's salary was considerably higher than Wendy's. He controlled the purse strings, and, in fact, financially at least, it was as if she were the child and he were the father. They both contributed to the household budget, however he had much more disposable income, which he spent on toys for himself. She knew nothing of his assets. He had a temper, was emotionally abusive, and occasionally even used physical force with her.

Wendy came to see me because she had been having an affair with a co-worker who was also married. She felt as though she were in love with him, but neither of them could picture ending their marriages. As I explored her feelings, it was clear that she did not love her husband, and felt little, if any physical attraction towards him. Physical intimacy happened rarely, perhaps only every two months. She could not see herself spending the rest of her life with him.

I asked her why she stayed in the marriage. It came down to the fact that she liked the lifestyle her husband's income afforded them. If they separated, her standard of living would decrease considerably. As she knew nothing of her husband's net worth, and because he was cunning enough to keep her in the dark, she did not feel she could count on getting much more than half of the equity in their home, and perhaps some spousal support for a few years at most.

When asked what she would do if her lover left his wife and wanted to be with her, she replied that she would leave her marriage.

In this case, ego has a strong foothold over Wendy's consciousness, and it is dragging her farther and farther away from her truth. The truth is, she is no longer in her marriage for love.

Soul says:

Love is the most powerful force in the Universe, and I feel my essence most fully when I am blossoming in the warmth of loving connection with another being. This relationship is no longer about love, and as long as

I am here, I cut myself off from the possibility of creating a life with one who honors my being, and is willing to co-create a life based on equality and integrity.

Ego says:
    I do not love this man, but I am scared to be alone. I do not want to have to watch my pennies. Even though I do not have much disposable income, at least I can pretend I am wealthier than I am because of what my husband has. I am afraid of moving to another state where he wants to go, because then I will feel trapped. I am terrified of staying with him, and terrified of leaving. Even though I tried to end my affair because I know it is wrong, I will probably keep it going because the love I feel is wonderful. I don't want to live without that. Maybe I'll just try to make the marriage sort of work for now, so I can continue to enjoy the material advantages, and then when something comes along that looks and feels good, I will leave.

Soul knows this is all wrong. It sees ego is manipulating to feed its own needs, and there will be much hurt. Soul knows these people must be honest with one another and deal with the issues between them. It is the only way they can be free. Either the truth will allow them to try to find a place where they can feel love again, or it will clearly illuminate their differences *so they can move on and find their true paths.*

Soulful responses are based on truth. They might include the following:
    "Dave, I am worried about moving, because I am un-

sure of my feelings for you. I hesitate to make a big change feeling as I do, and I think its only fair to let you know before we move."
or:
"There are aspects of our marriage that are not working for me. Before we go any further, I feel we need to explore those to see if changes are possible. I am not sure how I will handle irreconcilable differences over the long term.
or:
"I am sad and worried about our relationship. I can't find my loving feelings for you. I enjoy the life we have, and would like us to be together to parent our children, but I also need to feel like an equal partner. I feel like a child in this relationship, and I think that prevents me from feeling attracted to you. If we could get help to transform some of those things, maybe the love would come back."

Soul knows the truth may trigger a process of more authentic communication. Maybe there are embers of love that could be rekindled with the fresh air of a new basis for the partnership. Soul also knows the truth may hasten the ending of the relationship.

Soul knows *either way is fine.* If there is enough to sustain the relationship, it will survive. If there is not, to pretend will only prolong the pain. If these individuals are not right for one another, or not good for each other, then it is time to move on, focus on healing, assess the learning, and make space for healthier relationships.

Soul recognizes, as it stands, the situation is out of integrity, and nothing good can come of that.

SERENA AND ALI

Serena and Ali had been together for fifteen years, married for twelve. They had been through some struggles, but were committed to their marriage. They had two young daughters. Serena was not working, and Ali worked from home. They shared many of the household duties, and Serena was as adept at the outdoor work as indoor work, so they contributed equally around the house.

Ali loved Serena very much, and wanted to be closer to her. Serena was more distant. She was angry with Ali because of decisions he had made in the past without consulting her. He once purchased a vehicle because it was a good buy, and he needed it for his work. Serena was not so unhappy that he bought it; for she saw the need, but was annoyed he did not check with her first.

Ali was, for the most part, the responsible one in the family. He would get up in the morning and make breakfast for the children, because Serena would often sleep late, claiming she was too tired to get up. Eventually Ali resented her for this, especially since some evenings she would be out late with her friends, and he felt she was taking advantage of his willingness to get the kids up, fed, and off to school. Serena would wake up later, and have a leisurely coffee and cigarette, while Ali would be in his office, dealing with the pile of paper that was always waiting.

What bothered him most, however, was the lack of physical intimacy in their marriage. Serena did not seem to care if they ever made love. She said she was just never in the mood. Once she got into it, she enjoyed it, but she would never initiate it, and often rebuffed Ali's advances. In therapy we had worked to sort out many of the issues that frustrated this couple, and they worked well at compromising and communicating. They were friendlier to one another, and now could laugh together. Still, they were not making love, so it was time to go deeper.

It seemed to Serena that Ali expected he should be able to have intimacy with her whenever he wanted. She felt as though it was an obligation, and he was upset with her if she was not willing. Consequently, she attempted to keep such a distance between them, hoping the issue would never come up. She would wait until he was asleep before going to bed. She would pull back if he even tried to put an arm around her, or touch her in any way. Ali assumed she did not love him or find him attractive. At other times, he thought he was being punished. The issue for Serena was her feeling that she did not have a choice. She felt if she showed him any affection, he would expect sex.

We resolved this aspect of the problem when Serena agreed she would not mind making love if she did not feel pressure. About once a week would feel okay for her. The plan was that Serena would be the initiator. She would decide when it would happen.

Ali could relax, because he knew at least once a week he would have the opportunity for the intimacy he craved. This worked well for a while, but Serena was still not happy. She realized she needed *emotional intimacy* throughout the week, and without that she could not jump right in to physical intimacy. Ali needed to connect with her; they needed to spend time together in ways they did before the children were born. Like many couples, once the children came, they forgot about one another, devoting all of their energy to work, home and children.

When we look at this situation from the perspective of soul and ego, it is clear the egos of these individuals were stumbling around looking for self-fulfillment. Neither was looking at what the other was needing.

Ali kept knocking at a door that would not open, and Serena

kept backing away, not wanting to give anything until she was satisfied her needs would be met. Both were frustrated, and vented this energy on issues about finances, childrearing, her family, his family, and who should cut the grass. Ego says, "You give first, then I will give." It is easy to see how this creates a stalemate.

His ego might say:
" What does a guy have to do to get a little sexual release around here?
or:
" Sex, what's that?"
or:
"What's your problem?"
Her ego might say:
"Is sex all you ever think about?
or:
" Think about it, why would I want to have sex with someone who doesn't care about me?"
or:
" You don't have time to talk with me, but suddenly you have time to make love?"
or:
" You'll never understand. You're a man."

Soul is not interested in stalemates. Soul always carries us in the direction of unity, of healing, and resolution. Soul says: *"Something is not right here. We started out in love, but have ended up someplace else. Let us speak from the deepest part of our own souls so we may recognize one another again. Let us each listen with our hearts, so we may be open to receive and embrace the essence of the other. That is what we came here to do."*

How could Serena and Ali speak to one another from that place in each of us that is soul?

It might sound like this:

Ali: "Serena, you know that I love you and want us both to be happy. I've noticed you don't seem to want me touching you, and you are not too interested in sex. There must be a reason for that, and I'd like to know if there is something I need to be doing differently. Because I care for you, and us, I am ready to listen with my heart, and will not argue with you or judge you for what you might say. What you are feeling is important to me."

Or: " Serena, I feel as though I've lost touch with you. You mean so much to me. I want us to be close again. Please help me to find my way back to you."

Serena: "Ali, I can see you are frustrated with the lack of physical intimacy in our relationship. I am having some strong feelings inside that are making me pull away. I am not feeling good in myself, and so I do not have good feelings to bring to you. Simply making love with you when I have these feelings is not the answer, for then I find myself resenting you. Do you think we could work together to sort out the things that are bothering me, so we can move into a more loving space?"

Or: "Ali, I know we are having a problem with intimacy. I don't know what the answer is, but I would like to work with you to make things better between us. Maybe if we could talk about what we need and want, without blaming each other for where we are now, we might find some answers."

Soul might also say: *There are times in any relationship where things get out of balance. We do not need to turn on each other. It just might be that this problem has presented itself in our lives because there is something we each need to see. Perhaps this is a challenge that, when mastered, will carry us to an even deeper level of love and intimacy than we would have had otherwise. Let's open our hearts and minds, allowing our highest wisdom to guide us, and see if we can create something beautiful out of this struggle.*

For individuals who choose consciousness, life becomes a process of evolution, growth and change. The same is true of relationships. No one is born totally evolved, and relationships do not achieve instant soulfulness. Even evolved individuals have unevolved moments, and even soulful relationships will suffer at times when ego pushes its way in and dominates interactions.

Ego reminds me of the dandelions that pop up in my garden. Even when you think you have dug one up, completely removing its entire root system, it has a stubbornly persistent way of growing back. Soulful relationship involves weeding out negative or destructive aspects of the untamed ego. It might be easier to see those areas in our partner, but we must first weed the garden of our own awareness. Doing so requires surrender and humility: these are the first steps on the path to taming ego.

JOE AND GLORIA

An evolving relationship may go through many different phases. It is also possible for a couple to go through these phases in dealing with a single issue. Consider the following scenario:

Joe and Gloria were out walking. Gloria had been feeling vulnerable and stressed due to several issues in her life, unrelated to their relationship. She mentioned these feelings to Joe, who listened quietly.

As they walked on, he changed the subject, and farther up the road he started kidding around with her. She became annoyed, and told him he was acting silly. Things got quiet, as she pulled into herself. They returned home, and he later found her lying silently on her bed. He tried to approach her, but she was upset with him, suggesting he did not care about her. Joe had no idea where this was coming from. He tried to hug her, but she pushed him away. He asked what it was that changed her mood, and she told him she was upset that he did not say anything when she shared her feelings during their walk. She told him he just is not there for her.

Joe became upset, because in his heart he *was* there for her. He felt the best thing he could do when she was sharing her feelings was to simply listen. He began to feel annoyed at being judged, when he was trying. Gloria became even more upset, angry even, because in her mind Joe was only making things worse.

Thinking things would only deteriorate if he stayed, Joe decided to go home. This was the last straw for Gloria. Not only was Joe not there for her, but when she was even more upset than before, he walked out and abandoned her! She sobbed into her pillow, thinking she must end the relationship because it was just too painful.

Meanwhile, as Joe drove home, replaying the evening in his mind, he grew more frustrated and annoyed. He loved Gloria deeply and she knew it. Whatever he did seemed to be the wrong thing. He was troubled by the fact that things could be going so well, and suddenly, without warning, Gloria became dissatisfied with him. This had happened so many times before. He knew his tendency to become frustrated and angry really set her off. She took it personally, but it only happened because he did not know what to do.

Neither one slept well that night. The next morning Joe called to see how Gloria was doing, but she was quiet and distant. He decided to give her some space, and did not call for the rest of that day, or the next. She called him that evening, very angry because he had not called. He just did not know what she wanted, and began to defend his actions. She challenged him, and he became upset again. They began to fight, and finally she hung up on him. Each went through the next day with a heavy heart, wondering what would happen with their relationship.

The following day Gloria called, and was more settled. She told Joe she would really like to talk with him, but she did not want to fight. She suggested they spend the next day together, doing some things they both enjoyed, leaving their differences aside. She reasoned that if they could get into a more amicable space, remembering what they enjoy about each other, it would be easier to talk. Joe agreed to this plan.

As they worked together in her yard the next day, Gloria felt emotional pain rising to the surface. When they took a break, she looked at Joe, and said she felt like she could cry for a week. He responded with tenderness, first holding her, and then suggesting she come inside lie on the couch. As she did this, he placed his hand over her heart, and she sobbed. These were gut-wrenching sobs, bringing up buried pain stored up over a lifetime. Joe just sat with her, encouraging her to let the pain come out. When the crying was done, she began to soften.

They returned to the gardening, and as she pulled weeds and planted flowers, she began to remember. She remembered how her mother always criticized her father. Her mother could never ask politely for what she needed, but would expect her father just to know. When he did not respond as she expected, she would become angry, blaming and distant. Suddenly Gloria realized she was living out her parent's pattern. She rarely told Joe what she was needing, or what she wanted from him. She had a picture in her mind of how she wanted him to respond to her, and when his behavior did not match that picture, she was first disappointed, then upset with him.

He seldom knew why she was upset. It reminded him of the unpredictability of his alcoholic father. Joe always stood up to Gloria when her feelings caught him off guard, because long ago he promised himself he would not let anyone push him around like his father did. Maybe he was a little hard on her, but he'd had enough of that in his lifetime, and would not put up with any more.

Gloria did not know why he reacted so strongly, but assumed he was controlling and only wanted to shut her down as her father used to do. She too had promised herself she would not let any man ever overpower her like that again.

Upon realizing she was reliving an old pattern unconsciously adopted, Gloria decided to take responsibility for her part in creating it. She walked over to Joe, telling him she had something important to say. She told him she was going to do things differently. She explained that she saw, now, how she never gave him a chance to be there for her, because she did not let him know what she wanted. She acknowledged with a good deal of humility that she had criticized and judged him unfairly, comparing him to an ideal in her mind.

She could see how she was inadvertently setting him up to fail, and she apologized for the unconscious part she played in that pattern. She asked him if he would work with her to teach her how to let a man know what she wanted in a way that would feel good for him.

Joe was completely overwhelmed with what he was hearing. He felt such a profound release at the prospect of her willingness to help him to be there for her, for he wanted that more than anything. He knew he had a good heart, and truly did not know why things were not working. He recognized his own dysfunctional behaviors, and now understood why they were being triggered.

The prospect of working together with Gloria, growing in love and deepening awareness brought joy to his heart. Gloria, too felt a release. Instead of focusing on Joe, and all that she felt might be wrong with him, she turned her attention to her own deep inner process. She accessed the painful places she was unconsciously wanting him to fix. She released him from that responsibility. By simply feeling her pain, without blaming Joe for it, she began the process of freeing herself from the constraints of her very determined ego.

As she let go of her defensive, protective, polarizing ego, settling in to the wisdom of her soul, Joe automatically did the same. Ego melts away in the presence of soul. No longer adversaries, they were then able to talk like coaches reviewing a game, understanding what each was triggering in the other, and how they kept themselves stuck. They made a commitment to clear communication, and to help one another when things were being triggered.

The rest of the day they discussed many different things unrelated to their issues, and both shared more deeply than was their usual pattern. They felt intimately connected, respectful of one another, and peaceful. They had reached a new level of relationship.

MAKING THE SHIFT

The above description reveals a shift from ego consciousness to soul consciousness that occurred in the space of a few days. Such shifts might occur in an instant, or take as long as a lifetime. Some people never experience such shifts, remaining forever trapped by ego.

In the case of Joe and Gloria, they had been struggling with the same issues for almost five years. Try as they might to resolve them, things would get better for a while, but the old patterns kept recurring. It was almost as though soul made promises that ego would not let personality keep.

When we are able to surrender ego, if only for a little while, it creates enough of an opening in consciousness for soul's perspective to register, and even realign our thinking. Such realignment has been called enlightenment, heart opening, or insight. Regardless of what you call it, once you have experienced it, it is as difficult to go back to the old, limited ego perception, as it might be to put the genie back into the bottle. We may slip back many times on our way to becoming firmly grounded at a higher level, but it is never quite the same as before, because now we realize when we are slipping back.

We are now *aware* of a difference between ego's perceptions and reactions, and soul's understanding. It becomes increasingly uncomfortable to be in the presence of our own acting-out ego.

CHOICE

In earlier chapters we talked about the importance of becoming aware of our ability to *choose* the perspective from which we interpret life events. It may be that intellectual knowledge of the ability to choose is insufficient motivation for shifting to a place of making conscious choice.

Over the years, clients have repeatedly told me that they intellectually *know* the principles of growth and the evolution of consciousness, but cannot consistently put this knowledge into practice. Relationship is a crucible in which impurities in consciousness are burned off, allowing soul consciousness to shine through. It is here that we undoubtedly feel the deepest pain of ego's manifestation in our lives, and see most clearly and directly the difference in outcome when we adopt soul's perspective.

Approaching people with compassion, understanding, and acceptance always feels good in the body. Our energy is expansive and open. The body feels calm and relaxed. Operating from a place of judgement, criticism, and polarity always feels bad in the body. Our energy becomes contracted, and the body feels tense. Ego may justify these feelings by blaming another, holding the adversary responsible for the feelings created in the body.

Stress-related health problems are blamed on the environment, when more often it is the way we react to the events and people in our lives that creates the problems. In relationship, often this very learning is at the core of our issues. If we resist the learning, pain and struggle continue. If we surrender to the learning, we begin to move forward, growing deeper in love.

In order for this growth to occur, both parties in the relationship must come to this place of surrender: surrendering dictatorship of the ego, relaxing into the softness of soul. If only one is surrendering, for a time this may be a powerful discipline for that person. Sometimes the surrender of one will eventually trigger the surrender of the other.

However, if one is moving increasingly to a soulful perspective, and the other remains firmly grounded in ego, the relationship cannot survive. It is like a painful scene from a movie I saw many, many years ago. A woman was in the midst of giving birth, when it became evident that there was a problem. The only way the mother could survive was if the life of the baby was surrendered. Because she was a devout Catholic, taking the life of the baby was not an option. What ensued was a few more hours of torturous pain, after which both the mother and baby died. Relationship is sometimes like that.

If one surrenders her growth in order to save the relationship, her spirit dies. The relationship is not then truly alive either. Sometimes honoring the soul of one means the relationship dies. Naturally and ideally, as much as possible should be done to save both—to honor the integrity of the individuals, and the relationship.

It is important to recognize that if one is entrenched in ego perspective, unable to make the shift to a more expansive level, that does not make the person bad, dysfunctional, or in any way less. We are all at different places in our learning and evolution, just as students in a school are at different places along their journey.

We would not judge students who are at an earlier grade or program level, or those who do not have the intellectual capacity to master higher levels of academic learning. If one claims a soulful perspective, yet expresses disdain for a partner who is not 'at their level', you can be sure ego is still operating because there is judgement implied.

While we need not judge an individual who, for example, gives her children a lot of freedom, we may nonetheless not choose her when we need someone to care for our child. It is not a matter of right or wrong, good or bad, but simply what works for us in our lives, and what does not.

Sometimes, despite our best efforts, a relationship simply is not working. It is said there comes a time when the pain of holding on becomes worse than the pain of letting go. When that time comes, the learning then is about how to let go.

LETTING GO

Everything in nature has its cycles, including human relationships. We make the mistake, in the first place, of thinking we can make something as dynamic as human relationship last forever. We are drawn to others with whom we initially share a similar level of consciousness, and if neither changes, the relationship may continue as it is.

If both change, and allow the changes and shifts to become a dance of energies, then both people grow, and the relationship deepens.

Each relationship has a natural lifespan, and an important learning for us at this point in our evolution is to understand and honor that lifespan. We all know couples who have stayed together for decades, even though there is no love or joy between them. The relationship fulfilled its purpose a long time ago. Then there are those who, at the first sign of trouble, walk away from the relationship, writing it off before they have even begun to access the learning that was there.

You have to know how long to attempt to artificially prolong a life that is ready to leave a body, and you have to know how long to persist in attempting to breathe life into a child who's life has barely begun. In terms of relationship, these questions require discernment, but on some level your heart already knows the answer.

Because we believe in the illusion of permanence, we are often devastated when we truly see it is time to let a relationship go. We do not know what to do with it then, but we have learned from others that the thing to do is to fight and be angry, creating a tangible reason to 'split up.' So we plow the relationship under, ripping up roots and destroying flowers that may have continued to bloom indefinitely in spite of, or because of our absence.

We do not need to do it that way anymore. When it is time to do so, we have to learn to part company with love and grace, deeply honoring the gifts of learning we received with our partner. Even a troubled, turbulent relationship has its gifts. Each relationship is another piece in the puzzle of our understanding of life, love, and purpose; and ignoring any of the lessons makes our learning incomplete.

We will continue to draw to us the lessons at any given level, until mastery is attained. Stubbornly refusing to 'see' what is being shown results in more intense lessons, and prolonged struggle. Sadly, many find it easier to stay in a place of struggle, than to allow the change that is trying to happen.

Sometimes the lesson is to release a relationship that is no longer loving. If, despite your best efforts, a relationship dishonors or is harmful to you, there is an important lesson there too. Do not linger too long once you have grasped it.

A relationship that recognizes soul is a powerful opportunity for learning and transformation. The concentrated combination of energies holds potential as a powerful catalyst moving us along the continuum from ego to soul consciousness.

Our purpose here on Earth is to evolve to the point where we can 'be' love and compassion. Relationships that bring out our highest qualities are gifts to the self, and to the world. That is the ultimate goal. It is not so much about a couple 'creating' this wonderful state of harmonious loving between them, but rather to allow their own loving essences to flow towards the other. For this to happen, there must be a surrender of the ego qualities. It is only then that the heart remains open, and loving energy flows. Only then can we deeply touch each other's soul, entering a level of relationship that is truly sacred.

TAKING THE LEARNING

It may take several different relationships to challenge and prepare us for a mutually soulful union. Each individual with whom we relate reflects different aspects of our being, and we, theirs. We know we are on a path of growth when we can look at past relationships and see where we had blocks and limitations. If we blame an old partner for all of the problems in that relationship, we are looking through ego's rear view mirror.

Ego does not like to admit to mistakes or limitations. If we are able to see, and even feel somewhat humbled by the unconscious thoughts and actions of our unaware ego, then we are looking through the wise eyes of soul. We have access to a higher perspective. Once you learn the correct way to swing the golf club, you may not always do it that way, but you may at least recognize when you are not. You may also see an improvement in your game with attempting a proper swing consistently.

Similarly, once we have accessed that higher perspective, we can see when ego pulls us away from it. We are learning to know the difference, and to recognize the consequences of leading from ego. This is a critical point in our personal evolution, because it is only when we have this knowledge that we are truly able to make the choices that have the potential to transform our lives.

Relationships often facilitate this process, for, as stated earlier, it is in relationship that we seem to be able to see the role of ego most clearly. Perhaps, because, more readily than children, friends or co-workers, an intimate partner will give immediate feedback about the effects of our words and actions.

If ego is blocking our growth, this will show up most intensely in our closest relationships. Pain and struggle will ensue. If ego wins, the relationship loses. If ego wins consistently (ours, theirs, or both), we lose the relationship.

Ego may put the blame on the partner the first time, and perhaps even the second time. Eventually, however, if we hear the same thing from different partners, we know we need to look at ourselves. A stubborn ego will decide that men, (or women) are all the same, and will hold the personality distant from any intimate relationships, and will not allow full trust or surrender.

If, on the other hand, feedback from interactions with others motivates us to look at ourselves, we are then able to see what ego is up to. When we begin to tame it, we set the stage for healthy, soulful relationships. It is said we attract those who are at a similar level. Ego-driven personalities attract other ego-driven personalities. As we become more soulful, we will attract more like beings into our lives, or bring out the soulfulness of those already there. This is the highest purpose and most profound possibility offered in intimate relationship.

EXERCISES

1. Think of your current or most recent relationship.
2. List the three most important issues that arise in that relationship.
3. Identify the role of your ego in those issues.
4. Identify a previous relationship that ended due to differences.
5. Identify the role of your ego in those differences.
6. For each of the issues in questions 2 and 5, write a statement illustrating a soulful perspective towards that issue.
7. Adopt those soulful perspectives for the next week in your current relationship, and notice what happens.

Chapter 9

EGO AND SOUL AT WORK

For early humans, 'work' was the work of survival. Finding food, shelter, and protection from predators was a full-time job. Males were biologically programmed for hunting and gathering—females, for nurturing their young. This is how the species survived.

The right brain, with its emotional, intuitive, holistic nature was the dominant brain hemisphere. Time was perceived as cyclical rather than linear, and was measured in seasons, days, seeds, and birth-death cycles. Nature was the tuning fork to which humans aligned themselves. As the species developed, and with the evolution of language, brain dominance shifted to the left hemispheric modes. Time was perceived as linear. With language and abstraction came the separation of mind from nature. This led, ultimately, to fragmentation in our lives.

With the massive developments in technology, and the concurrent economic and social impact, fragmentation has increased further, and is generally accepted as 'the way life is.' In modern society we have food, without needing to plant or harvest; education happens in sterile classrooms; employees commute to their place of work; people stay connected via telephone or computer rather than family or community celebrations or rituals; and often spirituality is just one aspect of our lives, rather than a force permeating all we do. Recent trends towards simpler living and accessing the more soulful aspects of our being reflect an evolutionary movement towards balance and wholeness.

It is just this sense of balance and wholeness that is so often missing in the modern world of work, and our relationship to it. As we continue to evolve in consciousness, we become increasingly aware of imbalances in our lives. As we become more soulful in our lives generally, and more aware of our ability to make choices that support personal and even global evolution, our work lives may come under some self-scrutiny. Some will feel moved to make significant changes in the work they do, and for others, changing the relationship to their work will be sufficient to create the alignment they are seeking.

CONTINUUM OF CONSCIOUSNESS AT WORK

The continuum of consciousness we have described in relation to individual thoughts, attitudes, and behaviors can also be applied to work. Some types of work or businesses are based solely on a desire to create profit—to make money. At the most ego-based end of the continuum we might find those who would do anything, legal or illegal, moral or immoral, just to make money. At the most soul-based end of the continuum we might find Mother Teresa and others like her, whose work is solely for the benefit of others, with no material remuneration of any sort entering into the equation. This is not to suggest we should all quit our day jobs and devote our lives to charity. The reality of our lives and our world is such that we must find a place along the continuum that works for us.

We are at a time in history when there is heightened consciousness about the impact of the way we live and work on the planet as a whole, and upon our own individual journey. An example that touches both is vegetarianism. An individual may become vegetarian for health reasons, and also because he does not believe in killing animals to support his own life. Further, he may not want to support destruction of rain forests so the land can be used for raising cattle, because of the impact upon the ecosystem. He may then choose not to work for a company that supports the beef industry. If he is passionate about his beliefs and feels moved from somewhere in the core of his being to make a difference, he may open a vegetarian restaurant, publish a vegetarian magazine, or do research on organic farming. For this individual, there would be an integration between how he lives, what he believes, what feels right for his soul, and how he makes his living.

In their book, *Living With Our Genes,* Dean Hamer and Peter Copeland suggest that as we age, we become less self-centered, more willing to help others, and even more spiritual. No doubt we also develop a heightened sense of accountability, if for no other reason than we have been here long enough to see the effects of the actions of individuals, corporations, and nations. These shifts may also be occurring in the population generally, as our species comes of age. We may ask ourselves questions now, which may not have occurred to previous generations, such as whether the parent company for which we work is exploiting third world workers, or whether we can, in good conscience, work for a company producing a product proven harmful to health.

One of the questions we ask ourselves then, is if the work we are doing is in alignment with the highest good of the species and the planet. Another question is the extent to which our work is in alignment with who we are. If our nature is to be outdoors, hiking, swimming, or working in the garden, and our work involves spending forty hours per week in a windowless office, there is going to be imbalance. If our soul joyfully expresses itself in creativity, be it drawing, painting, music, or writing, and we work at an assembly line job, or spend the days entering data on a computer, we will not thrive. One who craves peace and solitude may feel stressed in a bustling workplace, and the 'social butterfly' may become depressed in an isolated home office.

A further dimension of the work issue is one that is not related to the work itself, but rather to the social and psychological environment in which we work. Is there a hierarchy, or are all workers of equal rank or status? Is there respect for others, and integrity in communications and processes? Do we feel inspired and supported, or discouraged and threatened? Every workplace is different, and while a workplace does not exist to fulfill our needs, the effects of our work and workplace upon our evolving being affect every area of our lives.

Both the individual and the workplace itself can be considered in terms of where each might be on the continuum of consciousness. An individual who is growing in consciousness may have an increasingly difficult time working for an employer or company that operates at a less conscious level. Let us look now, more specifically, at how these various dimensions relate to the continuum of consciousness.

Recall that ego defines itself in relation to the environment. The ego-based individual might define himself in terms of his occupation. "I am a doctor", "I am a teacher", "I am a computer technician", or "I am a stay-at-home-mom". This is different from saying, "My name is Susan, and I practice Family Medicine."

There is only a subtle difference in these ways of expressing what we do, but the impact can be profound if our identity is too tied up in what we do. If it is, then who are we if we no longer do that work? And who are we if our work does not reflect who we are at the level of soul?

Imagine the individual who loves hiking in the mountains, and spends every weekend doing just that. Where does his soul go as he sits in front of his computer from Monday to Friday? We may honor our souls on the weekends, but if our job is out of alignment with our souls, we have to realize we are spending a very large percentage of our time away from soul's path.

If our hiker sets up a business where he takes groups on hiking expeditions, then there is greater alignment between who he is, and what he does. Granted, it is not always economically feasible to make a living doing what we love, but it is possible to think about work that has some connection to who we are and what we love to do. A teacher may be passionate about teaching, and at work she is on her path. An artist may be content in his studio earning half of what he could make as a salesman. He is on his path.

There are growing numbers of employees, however, who are unhappy in their work, and would quit tomorrow if they won the lottery. They are not on their path, and their lives are fragmented. When they go to work, they have to slip out of their true selves, and take on a role that does not fit. This is soul-numbing. It is not surprising to me when these individuals develop depression, anxiety disorders, or health problems.

Ego drives them to continue along an unhealthy path, for fear of losing the identity they have developed in their occupation, fear of losing financially, or the fear that they cannot be successful in another field of work. So often I have heard people say they would leave their hated job in a minute, except for the fact that it pays so well. I ask what they would do if they did not need the money. Then they tell me their soul's desire.

As we tune in more to our souls, we come to recognize that our lives are a valuable resource, which we can use to make some contribution to our world, rather than just 'getting' for ourselves. Yes, we need to survive, but we also need to be conscious of how we are using our time on Earth. Are we doing what we do because of a clear and conscious choice, or are we doing it because of habit? What does soul want? To what extent will we allow ego to deny soul?

WORK AS A CONTEXT FOR EXPRESSING OUR HUMANESS

The workplace is a microcosm of the world. There we encounter individuals with whom we are connected neither by birth nor choice, but with whom we spend more time than friends or family. We can stop dating a partner, or stop seeing a friend, but unless we quit our job, we cannot divorce our co-workers.

There are often constraints around what we can express at work as well. If we blow our top we could get fired. Often work is a major source of stress in the lives of individuals, but there seems to be no choice other than to hold it inside until we get away from the job and can vent to whomever might listen.

The work setting can trigger all of ego's insecurities. Psychologically, it might remind one of being a child, with the boss as parent, and co-workers as siblings. The inner teenager may rebel against rules and policies. The inner child may have a sense of unfairness when someone else is promoted. Co-workers may gossip about and align against other workers, or management.

Clearly these are not mature adult behaviors, but they happen often. The only explanation is that the work situation has triggered a slide backwards on the continuum of consciousness, and ego-based consciousness becomes dominant.

In part this may be a result of the fragmentation in our lives, wherein we give up some of our autonomy as individuals in order to benefit from the specialization in society. If we work for someone else and make money, then we do not have to chop our own firewood or grow our own food. If this exchange is recognized and we enter into the agreement consciously and willingly, we can support the status quo. If we choose to work for ourselves, we can be the boss, but no one else will hand us a paycheque.

Ego-based consciousness does not see the big picture, or the way in which our own choices have resulted in our position in the workplace. If the individual is unhappy, ego will focus attention on everyone and everything else. The company is to blame, the supervisor is to blame, or the co-workers are to blame for the dissatisfaction.

Soul-based consciousness understands how we have created our own reality, and that if we want something different, we must be proactive in creating it. Ego expects the world to support and fulfill its needs, and to be fair. Soul-based consciousness recognizes if we have compromised who we are and what we came here to do for the sake of money, power, or status, then we will not be happy in our work. It also recognizes that the way we handle situations and people at work says more about where *we* are on the continuum of consciousness than about others.

Fellow workers are as much part of our tribe as friends and family. Ideally, it would be nice to belong to a highly evolved tribe, but sometimes our own evolution can be enhanced when we strive to remain soulful in the midst of ego-energy.

Consider our diagram in Chapter Three outlining the path to soulful living. If our relationships and experiences in the workplace are characterized by judgment, confrontation, blame, resentment, competition, impatience, and adversarial situations, we can be certain ego is operating. If those relationships and experiences are characterized by non-judgment, helpfulness, encouragement, patience, wisdom, connectedness, and harmony, then our work situation and our own responses are more soulful.

As we continue to evolve, we will see leaders who bring soulfulness to their organizations. We will see more companies emphasizing integrity in all of their dealings with employees, customers, and the world. The janitors will be valued as much as the president: the mailroom clerk as much as the executives. The understanding will emerge that it does not matter what our role or status is, what really matters is how we treat others, and where we are on the continuum of consciousness. Soulful employees will find soulful companies. Slowly things will shift.

MAKING ALL WORK SOULFUL

Naturally it is one thing to talk about creating soulful companies, or changing jobs to ones that honor soul, and another thing to do it. We are living in transitional times, so things may not change as quickly as we would wish. Sometimes jobs are scarce in some fields, or geographical areas. It may be that financial demands of our current situation make it impossible to make a shift. How then can we make our work life a soulful experience?

If Victor Frankl, author of *Man's Search for Meaning*, could make a soulful experience out of his time in a concentration camp, we can do it at work! It just depends on how we choose to look at it. I remember once being wheeled into the operating room at 7a.m. for a biopsy. On one level I was frightened and anxious. I might have seen the shiny walls and metal tables as cold and impersonal, and thought of myself as just another body going under the knife.

Instead, another perspective filled my consciousness. I realized that in that moment, the entire hospital facility, medical knowledge, the surgeon's training and nurse's expertise came into a concentrated focus, like a laser beam, for the purpose of my healing. The work of thousands of individuals, from architects to construction workers, from teachers and professors to scientists and administrators, from cleaning staff to delivery people forms a chain in which humanity works to help one another.

As the nurse spoke to me, I could see only her brown eyes looking out from her green surgical garb. I saw the beauty of her soul. In fact, I only saw her soul. The nurses, the anesthesiologist, even the surgeon, appeared to me as beautiful souls, dressed up as medical personnel. It was astounding to me how the Universe had organized itself completely and perfectly, so at the moment I needed to be healed, the entire system was there for me.

Prior to surgery, my surgeon was ninety-eight per cent certain the lump was cancerous. The biopsy came back clear. What, exactly, did those souls do while I was unconscious?

Think of a hospital job. Work can either be a routine process of going through the motions and collecting a paycheque, or the employees can see themselves as an extension of the healing energy of the Cosmos. I had been in operating rooms before, but the moment I was wheeled in to the one described above, I instantly felt the energy. Is it always there, in all things, and was I seeing it for the first time, or was it the brown-eyed nurse, who was very much into her soulful nature, who transformed the entire experience? Perhaps a little of both.

When I was young, while attending day camp one summer,

I slipped by the pool, banged my head, and was unconscious for a few minutes. I missed a few days of camp due to headaches. When I returned, the camp administrator called me into her office to welcome me back, and to see if I was okay. She was just doing her job, but something else happened.

I felt myself surrounded with a love and compassion deeper than anything I had ever felt. She looked beautiful and radiant, and the glow around her seemed to envelop me too. I have never forgotten that experience, yet it was likely no more than five minutes, years and years ago. She too, had brought her soul to work.

In hindsight, I believe she was delivering into my consciousness important information about bringing compassion to others along the way. It was filed away, but rose to the surface years later, when I began working with children.

Our work may simply be the context that brings us into contact with others who need to receive the gifts of our soul. The kind smiles and genuine helpfulness of a server at a restaurant may mean more to the diner than the server could imagine.

A lovely lady I know who is a widowed senior went to rent some scaffolding so she could paint her exterior windows. She planned to take it home, set it up herself, and get the job done. The young man who served her insisted on taking the scaffolding to her home himself, ensuring that it was set up properly. The joy and gratitude she felt at his kindness still radiated from her being as she told me the story. Just think of the positive energy he passed to her, and she then passed to all with whom she related the incident. I believe it was Mother Teresa who suggested we do small things with great love. Like a small pebble tossed into a large pond, the ripples continue on in an ever-expanding circle.

These are nice stories, and likely we could all find it in our hearts to do similar things. The real challenge comes when we are in a toxic work situation. Perhaps someone is negative towards us, or is a very difficult person with whom to deal. It is easy to get drawn into negativity ourselves. Even if we do not act it out in the work setting, we may find ourselves inwardly judging or outwardly gossiping to others. In this way we contribute to putting out ripples of negative energy.

I have come to think of what I once may have considered negative people or situations as opportunities to expand my capacity for loving compassion. It is easy to love sweet, cuddly innocent babies; it took Mother Teresa to show us the face of God even in those lying filthy and diseased in the gutters. Repulsiveness resides in our consciousness, not in the individual or situation that triggers it.

I have come to regard difficult people in the work situation as challenges to my soulfulness and professionalism. The more negativity I feel being triggered, the deeper I drop into love. I see the individual as hurting, and cut off from the light of awareness, and from his or her own soul. I respond the same way to that person as I would to one for whom I have deep admiration and respect. This does not mean that I try to become close friends, or start doing nice things for them, as they may not know how to receive that kind of energy.

It is okay even if someone does not like us. We may be triggering something that is hard for them to handle. If we respect all souls and their journeys, we give them the freedom to feel how they feel. If we are holding a space of integrity, and are not adding negative fuel to the fire, the situation usually becomes benign.

It can be incredibly healing when we remain in positive space even when someone is reacting negatively to us. It may cause them to quietly reflect on their own negative emotions, after which they tend to tone them down. This is actually the deepest respect we can give to the soul of a person whose ego is out of alignment, for we are looking past whatever is happening at the level of ego, and honoring the soul.

Work sometimes provides an excellent opportunity for movement along the continuum from ego-based to soul-based thinking and responding. We may have no choice but to be involved with the same people, on a daily basis, perhaps over a period of years. Consequently, it is hard to escape the lessons being offered.

There is much to think about in terms of ego and soul in the workplace. For most of us, it is enough for now to be conscious of the fact that a job is not just a job. It is another opportunity for growth. What we do, where we do it, and how we do it are variables with infinite permutations and combinations. The nuances of those merit reflection, especially for those of us for whom work constitutes a large portion of life.

EXERCISES

1) In what ways is ego directing your work life? What ego needs are being fulfilled?
2) What role does soul play in your work? In what ways is soul satisfied in your work?
3) What ego reactions are triggered at work?
4) Which soul interpretations (understanding, compassion, acceptance) might heal those reactions?
5) If your soul could choose your work, what would it be?
6) List changes you could make so that work could be a more soulful experience.

Chapter 10

BRINGING IT ALL HOME

If you are still reading, by now you should have a pretty good sense of the difference between ego-based consciousness and soul-based consciousness. You are also likely developing a sense of where you operate from in various situations.

The first step in transformation is understanding the continuum of consciousness and behavior, for understanding the continuum implies recognition that there are different ways of thinking and responding.

The next step is *choosing to make a choice*. One can have all of the understanding, and an ability to eloquently talk the talk, yet continue to allow ego to produce reactive thoughts and responses. When we decide to recognize the possibility of choice in any situation, we are becoming aware and conscious. When we choose soulful responses, then we are evolving. When we *are* soul, we are enlightened.

In choosing an evolved path, our goal is to increase our experiences of enlightenment: to practice enlightened behavior. Like blossoming flowers, we lean towards the light and grow in that direction. We do not completely merge with the light. That comes later.

If we watched home movies taken when we were three or four years old, we might see ourselves being unwilling to share, hitting a child we did not like, or throwing a tantrum when we did not get our way. We might feel a little embarrassed, but thankful we grew past that stage. We understand we did not know better then.

But what if a camera caught us as adults, in one of our less evolved moments? What if *that* were shown on national television? We would be highly embarrassed because we *do* know better. Once we have awareness, there are no excuses.

Imagine now, that when we leave this Earth, we debrief with other evolved souls, and must watch the cosmic equivalent of home videos. How will we account for allowing ego to run roughshod through our lives and the lives of others at a point when *we could have chosen* differently?

Will we regret having become so wrapped up in ego's dramas that we missed the beauty, depth, and perfection of life, and the opportunity for soulful connections with others? Will we be like the workaholic who, on his deathbed, realizes he sacrificed his soul to work — only it will be to ego that *we* sacrificed *our* souls?

I was ten years old when I realized I could absorb wisdom if I really listened to my Grandmother. Prior to that realization, I had tuned out when she started to tell me things she thought I should know. It occurred to me that I might save myself a lot of difficult learning if I could take the wisdom that grew out of her difficult experiences. I understood her desire to pass on her insights and truths. It is what the elders have always done for the good of the tribe, and what we do when we truly love and care for another.

This is what soul wishes to do. Soul understands ego's limitations, but would dearly love to assist in the evolutionary journey. The human heart/mind is like a bridge: a bridge that can be a channel for ego, or for soul. What we choose to bring in through consciousness and express out into the world *is up to us.* If we want to make a forward shift, we first need to know *where we are* currently, and where we are aiming to be.

The next section will provide illustrative examples with real situations, from three perspectives. The first perspective will be ego-based, the second will be ego-on-the-way-to-soul consciousness, and the third will be soul- based consciousness. Reading through them will help you to place yourself on the continuum of consciousness. Naturally, we can be at different places at different times in our lives, and in different situations. The goal is to move all of our perceptions, responses, and behaviors towards the soul-based end of the continuum.

A MATTER OF MONEY

1) **Ego-Based**—Joe likes money. He never has enough. He stole a purse out of a woman's grocery cart. It contained ninety-five dollars. To him, it was a windfall. He went out that night and celebrated, buying beer for all his friends.

2) **Evolving** –Joe would never steal from anyone. That's just wrong. However, when making a purchase one day, the clerk gave him too much change. Joe pocketed the money, feeling it must be his lucky day. A big chain store would never even miss ten dollars, he reasoned, so it wouldn't be hurting anyone.

3) **Soul-Based**—Joe was walking through the fairground, and found fifty dollars lying on the ground. If he did not pick it up, someone else would. He picked it up, and began to think of who might have lost it. Perhaps someone had saved for months to bring his or her children to the fair. If he took it to the lost and found, maybe the attendant would just keep it. Joe de-

cided to turn it in anyway. He wouldn't feel right spending someone else's money, and this way, the person who lost it would have some chance of getting it back if they did decide to check the lost and found.

WHAT IS THE TEACHER TEACHING?

Sharon had been teaching grade two for fifteen years. Sometimes it was hard to remain patient. Class sizes were steadily increasing, and with new low-cost housing built near the school, they seemed to be getting children with more problems. Take Lenny, for example. He could hardly read, and was always disrupting the class. His Mother was a single parent with two pre-schoolers, and didn't even seem to care about Lenny.

1) **Ego-Based** – Sharon really didn't like Lenny. The other kids knew it, but how could you hide it? He was always in trouble. Her job would be so much easier if he were not in her class. Maybe if the principal could see how bad he was, they'd put him in a special class. She wasn't about to waste a lot of time with him. Every time he misbehaved she sent him to the principal. If he wasn't doing his work, she would send him out in the hall. He wasn't learning anything in class anyway. None of the kids liked him either. He just didn't belong in her class. Why couldn't anyone see that?

2) **Evolving** – Sharon liked her class this year. Except for Lenny. She knew she shouldn't dislike a child, but he could be so irritating. He obviously wasn't getting much at home. She would talk to the principal about getting some extra help for him. She'd make sure to give him work he could handle, so he wasn't so distracting. She'd have to watch the other kids too, because he could easily become the class scapegoat. She resigned herself to the fact that she might not be able to do much

for him, but she'd do what she could, and next year he'd be someone else's problem.

3) **Soul-Based** – Sharon could see immediately that Lenny had some problems. Poor kid. His dad walked out leaving his Mom with two preschoolers. She must be overwhelmed.

Sharon would make a point of getting to know her. They just moved in to the new low-cost housing, so she probably didn't know anyone, and the school might be her only real contact with the outside world.

Sharon knew it would be hard for Lenny to fit in. He *was* different. She decided she would enlist the whole class to make sure Lenny had a good year. She made him a helper right away, and without directly mentioning Lenny, she spent a lot of time talking with the class about the importance of supporting and helping one another. The class knew that Lenny was important to Sharon. They saw how kind she was to him, even when he misbehaved. They also responded to him with patience, and a few even took him under their wings. They protected him on the playground, and showed how proud they were of his progress, however slow. Sharon had worked with an educational specialist to design a program for him, and he was progressing well. Sharon was delighted that her class had learned to be non-judgemental and supportive. Lenny was a great teacher for all of them.

AN ISSUE OF TRUST

Blake was late getting home. Mary was feeling insecure and worried about the relationship. She questioned Blake about where he was.

1) **Ego-Based**—Blake began yelling at Mary and pushing her around, because he was not about to have some woman nagging him or trying to control him. He told her he would do

whatever he pleased, and if she did not like it, she could just leave, because he was not going to change.

    2) **Evolving** – Blake sensed Mary's jealousy. He became a bit defensive, and hurt that she would question his integrity. He pulled away from her a little, and even questioned the relationship. He did not like it when women got all suspicious. He did love her though, so decided to let it go.

    3) **Soul-Based**—Blake sensed Mary's fear, and realized she was extra sensitive because her last partner had cheated on her for months prior to announcing he was leaving. He sat her down, took her hand and looked straight into her eyes. He told her he understood why she was worried, but needed her to know how much he loved her, and that he would never do anything to jeopardize their relationship. Further, his own sense of integrity would not allow him to violate the trust they shared. He also invited her to seek his reassurance anytime the worries resurfaced.

A LITTLE WHITE LIE

Tracey cancelled her plans to see a movie with Karen saying she did not feel well. Karen went out with friends, and saw Tracey across the street, in a coffee shop with Dave.

    1) **Ego-Based** – Karen marched across the street and confronted Tracey in the coffee shop. She yelled at her, calling her a low-life scumbag, and told her never to call again.

    2) **Evolving** – Karen felt hurt and betrayed. She called Tracey the next day, saying she was angry and upset, and could not believe Tracey could have lied to her. She told Tracey that since the relationship obviously meant so little to her, she was not sure if she could still be friends.

    3) **Soul-Based** – Karen met Tracey for coffee. She told her that she valued their friendship, and was aware of what hap-

pened the other night. She told Tracey that truth and honesty were very important to her, and she would rather Tracey tell her when she wants to change plans, even if it might be disappointing, than to feel she has to protect Karen from the truth. Karen assured her of her caring that she would certainly have understood if Tracey felt a need to meet with Dave. Even if Tracey did not want to spend as much time with Karen, she would understand and accept that too. Karen explained that to her, friendship or relationship are not about duty and obligation. All parties must be free to speak and act according to their truth. She also reassured Tracey that she was choosing not to be angry or resentful, and looked forward to continuing the relationship with openness and a higher level of trust and honesty.

OOPS, I FORGOT

Marion's son, Brian, was a bit of an absent-minded professor, completely wrapped up in his job. When he was in town, he showed her how much he loved her, but in-between times he often went for weeks without calling. This year, for the second year in a row he forgot her birthday completely.

1) **Ego-Based** – Marion felt hurt and rejected. She called her daughter to complain about Brian's selfishness. She told her friends too, who agreed that adult children can be so self-centered. Some suggested Marion should reduce his share in her will. She considered it. When Brian finally did call, Marion was cool and distant. Brian did not know what was up with her, and only found out when he called his sister to inquire.

2) **Evolving** – Marion felt hurt and rejected. She kept her pain to herself, putting on a happy face for her friends and her daughter. She secretly felt Brian was very selfish, and thought sometimes she did not even like him. His father, whom she

divorced years earlier, was like that too. Maybe it's a genetic thing. She decided not to say anything or show her disappointment, because she did not want to create an issue.

3) **Soul-Based** – Marion realized Brian loses track of dates and times. Even though he is extremely bright, and good at his technologically complex job, the simple things in life seem beyond his grasp. One year, he forgot her birthday, and felt bad afterwards. The next year, Marion telephoned Brian ten days before her birthday, and told him to please not worry about it, since birthdays are really not a big deal to her, and she knows he loves her. That's all that matters. Brian smiled to himself, realizing his Mom, as usual, was thinking about the feelings of others more than her own. She did not want him to feel bad again this year. After hanging up the phone, he called the florist while it was fresh in his mind, and arranged for flowers to be delivered to Mom on her birthday.

YOU CAN'T SAY THAT TO ME

"I hate you!" Becky screamed at her Father. She was angry because he had agreed she could go to Sue's party, and now he changed his mind. Just because he found out Sue's parents were out of town, he wouldn't let her go. She was sixteen, and was tired of being treated like a little kid.

1) **Ego-Based** – Joe was sick of Becky's attitude. She was getting so mouthy, just like her Mother. "Well I hate you too, so we're even," he mocked. "You can hate me even more, because your mouth just cost you your soccer registration fee. See if I do anything for you again! You're just like your Mother. No wonder I divorced her." Becky ran from the house, slamming the door behind her, thinking to herself that she really did hate him. She was running away. She could stay at Sue's. Nobody cared about her anyway.

2) **Evolving** – Becky's words really stung. Joe knew he had to nip this in the bud, or he'd just get more and more of it. He told Becky what she said was the worst thing a child could ever say to a parent. After all he had done for her, and being a pretty good father all those years, her words showed her complete lack of respect or appreciation. It saddened him to have raised a child who was capable of saying such a thing. He told her he still loved her, and would continue to be the best father he could, but those harsh words would echo in his consciousness for the rest of his life. He also told her she was grounded for a week. Becky felt so guilty that she did not argue. She crawled into bed, and pulled the covers over her head. She thought about what a loser she was. She didn't even care about the party.

3) **Soul-Based** – When Joe heard those words he realized Becky was hurting badly. Of course she would be mad. The kids planned this party and were excited: their first real party with no adults around. Joe knew Becky didn't hate him, but just could not handle the frustration of having her plans blocked this way. Joe remembered his own frustrations with his parents, and how hard it was sometimes to be a teenager.

He knocked gently on Becky's door. He could see she'd been crying. He hugged her, and told her he needed to explain a few things. He reminded her of their long-standing rule about not being in friend's houses when no parents were home. More importantly though, was the fact that Sue's parents would be extremely upset if they knew what Sue was planning. He also explained how fast word gets out when there is a party where parents are out of town, and how uninvited guests can show up. Fifteen people may be invited, but fifty could arrive. Things can get out of hand, and the home could be vandalized. Even though Sue invited Becky, if damage occurred and Sue's parents took legal action, Becky could be considered a trespasser.

He reassured Becky he loved her very, very much. It was

hard having her so upset with him, and he wanted her to enjoy her teenage years. Sometimes though, a parent has to take an unpopular stand. He really wanted her to understand that violating someone's home is not acting with integrity, and even if Sue's parents were okay with it, he would still consider the situation too risky. His job, until she was eighteen, would be to provide protection and guidance. That's what Dads are for. He laughed telling her it's one of those hard jobs that someone has to do. He said he hoped she would not hate him for too long, because he sure loved her. She hugged him and apologized. She told him to never believe her if she ever said she hated him, because she really loved him, and he was a great dad.

MARRIAGE BREAKDOWN

Diana and Ben were high school sweethearts. They married young, and Diana worked for the first five years so that Ben could finish law school. They had two children, and once they were in school, Ben urged Diana to go back to work. Two years later, he announced he was leaving the marriage. He had found someone new. Diana was devastated.

    1) **Ego-Based** – Diana became bitter, and decided to make things as difficult as possible for Ben. She called everyone they knew, including his family, and told them that Ben was cheating on her. She told her children that Daddy did not love the family anymore, and was going to live with another woman. She fought for custody of the children, and then made access difficult for Ben. She told the children that Dad's girlfriend broke up the family and so they should not ever be nice to her. She never let them forget that Ben had ruined all of their lives.

    2) **Evolving** – Diana was crushed, and begged Ben to stay. She could not imagine life without him. She told him she could never make it on her own, and would do anything to keep him

there. She felt worthless and unattractive, and did not think she would ever find a good man who wanted to be with her. She became depressed as she imagined living the rest of her life alone, with nothing really to live for. She reluctantly agreed to shared custody of the children, but deeply resented the time the children spent with their Dad. She never said much, but the children always knew she was sad when they left, and felt guilty for leaving her alone.

3) **Soul-Based** – Diana was in shock. She had pictured growing old with Ben. She could not believe her life had taken this turn, and she was filled with grief. She realized Ben must not have been happy in the relationship, or he would not have become involved outside the marriage. She had not been so happy with it herself, but they had been together a long time, and besides, she was so involved with the children that it did not seem to matter that much. Actually, she saw herself doing what her Mom had done. Isn't that how it is after a certain number of years? Now what? She knew people who got divorced, and recognized in time they all got on with their lives. Come to think of it, some seemed pretty happy now. Still, this was a crisis, and her thoughts turned to how they would explain this to the children. She decided to go for counselling, so she would have some support through the process, and to gain some guidance about how to handle the children.

Eventually she and Ben were able to talk calmly about the fact that they had married so young, and had really grown apart. They were thankful for the years they shared, and would do it again the same way, for they could not imagine the world without their beautiful children in it. They worked out a co-parenting arrangement, and the children adjusted well. Eventually she remarried, and the children reaped the rewards of two families who loved them dearly.

DOWNSIZED

Eighteen years had passed since Eric began his career with the telephone company. It was hard to believe he was forty years old. The years had been good. His children were teenagers now, so the next ten years would be busy, getting them through school and college. His wife worked part time, just to get out a bit. Their plan was to retire shortly after he turned fifty. He would have a decent pension, and if he kept up his savings plan, they would be in good shape. He was totally unprepared when the managers were called into the vice president's office and told that due to downsizing their positions were being eliminated. He did not really hear the details of the package being offered, and felt like a criminal when each of the managers was accompanied to his office to remove his belongings, return keys, and then escorted out of the building.

1) **Ego-Based** – Eric was angry. He could not believe that after eighteen years of good service, this was the thanks he got. He felt betrayed by his supervisor, who he thought was his friend. What a conspiracy! He headed for the bar, and the more he drank, the angrier he got. Eventually he dialed his supervisor from his cell phone, and released a string of slurred expletives. When he got home he yelled at everyone, grabbed a beer and sat in front of the television for the rest of the evening. He didn't really see anything, for he kept running things through his mind. He felt like a loser, and wished he could do something to that smug supervisor who was secure in *his* job, and probably got a raise to boot. The next day he was still angry, and announced to his family that things would be different. He told his wife to get out and get a full-time job, and told the children they better think about getting jobs too, because there was no way he would be able to pay for college now.

2) **Evolving** – Eric was in shock. He drove home, thinking

this was just a bad dream. He kept playing things over in his mind, and it just didn't seem fair. Surely they could have found other positions for the managers. He worried for his future. Yes, the package would help in the short run, but he couldn't retire at forty years old. Who would hire a forty year old? He was scared. This was the worst thing that had ever happened to him. What would his friends and family think? His buddies were all doing so well. Maybe he should have gone into engineering as he first planned. He felt as if he'd just been fired. Over the next weeks he became depressed, feeling like a failure. Everyone tried to cheer him up and encourage him. His wife even offered to work full time. He began hating himself, and feeling like a nobody. When you meet someone they always ask what you do. What could he say? Friends told him to just look for something else, but he didn't even have a resume. Never thought he'd need one. Finally he went for counselling, because it was part of the package. Slowly he came to terms with the situation, and eventually got hired by another company. He invested most of his package, because he feared this might happen again.

3) **Soul-Based** – Eric was stunned. He had heard about downsizing in big, international companies, but never thought it would happen in his company. He knew he needed an action plan. His wife and children had always felt so secure, and he did not want them worrying about this turn of events. He understood that middle management is the first to go, so he didn't take it personally. Wow, that must have been so hard for Dave, his supervisor. He must feel terrible. Eric decided he'd call him later. He valued his friendship, and wasn't about to hold this against him. It wasn't Dave's fault. Eric reflected that he had been feeling bored in his job, and had often wondered how he'd get through another ten years. He had been trading off job satisfaction for financial security. Maybe the Universe was just

giving him a little nudge. There could be an up side to this. The package was enough to cover things for eighteen months, so he could actually manage not working for quite a long time. He couldn't see himself sitting around that long, but it was nice to know he didn't have to panic. There was time to figure something out. He could go back to school, or he could think about starting his own business as he'd often dreamed. He decided he was going to consider this an opportunity rather than a setback. It was important to show his children a good model for handling the unexpected. He called his wife, saying he wanted to take the family out to dinner to that quiet place they often chose. After hearing about everyone's day, Eric made his announcement. He told his family that an interesting opportunity had been presented to him. He said that after eighteen years of doing the same thing, it was time to create a new career for himself, and he wished to discuss some possibilities with them. Of course they were curious, but all began suggesting possibilities, some of them quite humorous. His wife then asked why, all of a sudden, he was thinking of changing careers. He then explained what had happened at work. He assured them that this kind of thing happens a lot, and will likely happen more and more. People just have to learn to adapt and move on. The children worried about his income, so he explained about the package, and that he did not expect their lives would change much. Even if he had been fired, and there was no package, Mom could work more and the kids could get after school jobs. The main thing was that they were all healthy, and together, as a family, they could handle whatever life brought their way.

SOUL-BASED LIVING

In these practical examples, the characteristics of ego-based and soul-based responding are evident. The ego-based responses are emotional and reactive. They involve judging another, and may involve confrontation, manipulation, or controlling behaviors. You can almost feel the tension that the individuals would be experiencing in each situation. It is clear how ego-based responding could become a self-perpetuating downward spiral, creating more negative energy at every turn. Every day could be a struggle.

The soul-based responses are characterized by understanding, compassion, and acceptance. In each case, there is a sensitivity to what others are feeling and experiencing. There is a balanced calm in each approach, and every person is valued and honored. There is no judgement, but only patience, trust, and kindness.

In each situation there is some learning, growth, and even healing. The communication is healthy, and in the end there is a sense of resolution, and even greater love and connectedness amongst those involved. The way life experiences are handled results in a deepening of loving connections. There is wisdom in the process, and a sense of peace and harmony.

Soul-based responding creates expanding spirals of positive energy, in turn creating optimism and satisfaction with life.

If the energy we create radiates outward, affecting others, it is clear how negative spirals could spread, almost like 'emotional viruses', contaminating relationships, organizations, and the larger environment. Expanding spirals of positive energy would be like fresh air, clearing away toxins and bringing health and vitality to individuals, groups, and ultimately the species.

With the understandings you have now gained about ego and soul, you are equipped to view any situation, and determine which perspective is operating. More importantly, you will find yourself becoming increasingly aware of your own responses, and the category into which they fall. As you continue to evolve, it will become more and more uncomfortable to watch your own ego reactions. It will eventually become uncomfortable to even entertain ego's thoughts!

As you quiet ego, you will begin to feel the energy of soul filling your consciousness. You will feel a sense of lightness. As your thinking and responding become more soulful, you will experience an increasingly relaxed flow in your life.

Ego-dominated situations that seemed normal before, will feel toxic. Eventually soul-based living will feel so natural, so obvious, and so simple. You will begin to see the purpose of life as something completely different than what ego led you to believe. Your work with ego is not quite complete, however. In the next chapter, we will learn how to guide ego through its ultimate challenge.

EXERCISES

1) Think of a difficult situation in which your ego reactions created pain. Write out what the script would look like for a soul-based response.
2) Look at your life currently, and identify issues around which your ego is still reacting. Make a list of these, and then write out the soul-based solutions.
3) Pick one of the above issues, and begin to implement a soul-based process. Note where ego objects to the idea of doing so. As you implement the process, pay attention to how ego gets triggered.
4) Practice remaining soul-based, even if others respond from ego.

Chapter 11

The Ultimate Letting Go

DEATH: NEMESIS OR TEACHER?

We have now followed ego from its most humble beginnings. A baby is born: a soul has manifested in human form. Ego develops to support physical survival. If the infant were not able to draw attention to itself—to demand fulfillment of its needs—it could perish. Ego is like the shell around the developing chick, the cocoon around the evolving butterfly, or the seed jacket around the potential blossoming flower.

If the shell does not crack, if the cocoon does not give way, if the seed jacket does not break open, then the inner potential goes unrealized. Soul will move on, whether or not it is expressed, but then the whole point of life will have been missed. That would be like arriving at a vacation destination, be it a beautiful paradise, a safari, or a spa retreat, but never leaving the airport once you got there. Before you know it, it will be time for your return flight, but you will not have done what you went there to do.

Eventually the uncracked shell, the unopened cocoon, or the intact seed jacket will disintegrate, the inner potential having been wasted. Nothing is permanent. Ego's agenda has been survival, pleasure-seeking and pain-avoidance. Like a child building a sand castle, ego creates the illusion of permanence, and becomes attached to the world it has created. It holds on tightly.

This goes against the natural process, thus creating struggle and pain. Upon surviving to adulthood, a natural evolution would see us gradually blossom into the fullness of our soul essence. Little by little, ego would fall away, revealing the unique potential within each of us. We each have our own way of expressing the Universal soul, which moves through us, and of which we are but one facet. At the same time, we would also experience connection with one another, recognizing that we *are* unique expressions of the *same energy.*

As we move through life, natural unfoldment would see us becoming stronger expressions of soul, releasing ego and its attachments. By the time of our physical death, the transition out of physical form and into pure spirit would be smooth, natural, and effortless. It does happen this way in many cultures, but is not the norm in the western world. Perhaps our over-development of ego makes the transition that much more difficult.

Nonetheless, as we become more evolved, we can have compassion even for our own egos. We must understand ego's perspective, if we are to consciously alter our own path. Let us now take a look at the journey of life through the eyes of ego.

Think of a little child with a leading role in a school play. Imagine he is the king in a fairly tale. Throughout the practices, and during the run of the play, he wears his luxurious robe and golden crown. Everyone refers to him as 'your highness'. He is so completely into the role that he actually feels like the king.

When the play is over, he must return the robe and crown to the wardrobe department. Nobody bows to him anymore, or calls him highness. In fact, after a few weeks most have forgotten about the play and his part in it. He is just another ordinary child, like everyone else out on the playground. He feels lost and confused. Something that had become so much a part of him and how he viewed himself, has slipped from his grasp. This is how ego feels about its own death.

In fact, this is how all of the cast members might feel as the play comes to an end. They have become comfortable in the role they play, and the relationship of their character to all of the other characters. Each loses his own role, and his relationship to all of the other characters.

The story depicted by a play ends at the same time for all of the characters. Not so in life. We each have our own story, which overlaps the stories of all of those living, and who have ever lived. We play different roles in many different plays, which run simultaneously. If one person dies, then one character is eliminated from many different stories. If it is a wife, husband, mother, father, or child, then many stories lose one of their leading actors. In life, the part cannot be assumed by an understudy. The play itself has to change to accommodate the loss.

If we were talking about plays with actors, and the process were one of evolving stories, with actors stepping in and out of roles, we would likely find the whole thing fascinating. We would be able to step back and observe the changes, accommodations, and new directions continually being created.

Perhaps the king would disappear from one play, and reappear in the part of a gardener in another. The beautiful Elizabethan maiden, who was the love of our life in the Shakespearean tragedy, might reappear as our daughter in a modern drama. Nothing would be constant except transformation itself. We could allow for fascination because of our acceptance of the changing nature of the process. Soul knows this is the nature of life. Ego does not.

Ego is like the little boy who played king. Ego becomes completely attached to the role, building upon it, embellishing it, and protecting it. Ego knows one day the play must end, but often spends a lifetime trying to avoid acknowledging the fact. The more props ego can construct, the more intensely ego gets into the role, the easier it is to maintain the denial and pretend the play is the reality.

Attachment to the 'story' grows increasingly stronger. The more powerful the attachment, the greater the pain when ego is awakened out of denial. Awakenings from denial are often rude ones, and, like an awakened sleepwalker, ego is often disoriented and confused. Someone dies, and ego's life collapses—or the physical body suffers a heart attack, and ego's sense of self and security collapses. Soul has compassion for ego's pain; but through the cracks created by suffering and disorientation, it also sees an opportunity for its own voice to be heard.

What is it all about? In truth, no one really knows. On another level, we all know. Let me explain. Recall our metaphorical story in chapter seven, where certain souls incarnated into distressed family systems to change the evolutionary pattern. Because the play was not working well, the script was changed, with new scenes and actors added.

Perhaps all of our life stories are plays that emerge as soul attempts to manifest in physical form. Think of soul as a basic element of the Universe, as water is a basic element on earth. Water changes form: sometimes the molecules and atoms exist as components of a liquid, and may manifest as an ocean, a dewdrop, a tear, or a waterfall. Sometimes it is solid, manifesting as an iceberg, an icicle, or an ice cube in your drink.

It can also seem to disappear completely, evaporating into nothingness, yet it is still there. It never really disappears, but continues to change form. As we know from quantum physics, even in its most solid form, any object is mostly empty space! In the case of a human body, if you eliminated all of the empty space, meaning the space between the molecules, atoms and quantum particles, what remains would fit on the head of a pin.

IMPERMANENCE

Imagine we are all ice cubes. Better still, imagine we are made of ice, but each of us has been carved into a unique shape by a master ice sculptor. We get attached to who we are, and we get used to those around us. From the moment we are formed, the process of evaporation begins. We do not think about that though, because we are busy building a story. We get so much into the story that we forget everything is temporary. We get clothes for our bodies, and build houses to live in. We do something to support ourselves, so that we can feed our bodies, clothe them, and provide shelter. We bond with others, and create offspring.

If one among us 'evaporates', we become extremely upset at having lost one of our cast members. Even if that does not happen, with middle age, we begin to realize our shape is changing—we are not as solid and well-formed as we once were. Panic can set in. Some gracefully adapt, while others may find specialists who reshape the body, sculpting a bit here and there, in an attempt to slow the disintegration process.

Imagine how vulnerable, insecure, and unstable we might feel if we were made of ice! How frighteningly impermanent!

Truth is, though, flesh and bones are just as impermanent. Ego has a huge problem with impermanence, and not being in control. So ego constructs a very solid story, and accumulates solid things with which to surround itself, in order to create some sense of permanence and control. Naturally ego becomes deeply attached to the story and the material things, for that is the only way it can maintain the illusion. Egos also bond with other egos: co-creating and sharing illusions make them all feel more real.

Soul, on the other hand, has none of these issues. Think of soul as the atoms or molecules of the ice. The shape, form or particular manifestation the atoms or molecules adopt in any given time or space really does not matter. Soul knows it *is* the cosmic dance. It can manifest in form, or be formless. It can drop into time and space, or transcend them both. Soul does not see itself as separate from anything: soul experiences oneness. Soul is the ocean, *and the* single drop. But even as a single drop, soul does not see itself as separate from the ocean.

Can you imagine how much of a struggle life might be for a drop of water that forgot its connection with the ocean? Separate and alone, it may well search out other drops, developing a deep attachment to some of them, attempting to recreate the loving oneness and sense of home from which it emerged.

It might keep its droplet boundaries pretty well defined, for fear of losing its very self. And yet, it is that sense of *being self* that has created the problem in the first place. *Being self* would not be a problem if it were seen as only a temporary emergence, but not disconnection, from the source or oneness. It is the disconnection that creates the struggle.

It was not meant to be this way. Yes, our souls have traversed from another dimension and have taken on temporary physical form; but like the stories of pilots who became disoriented in the Bermuda Triangle, and assumed their perceptions were real and their instruments were wrong, we have lost track. Our hearts are our automatic pilot, programmed with greater wisdom than our mere minds could ever construct. The mind can certainly be used in the service of soul, but for most, it has been taken over by ego. If we have not learned to be guided by our heart's wisdom, or if we discredit that form of knowing, then we plunge into a sea of unconsciousness.

If we align with ego, we must prepare for a rough ride, because eventually ego will crash. If we align with soul, all struggle ends, for we have perfect understanding.

Perfect understanding does not necessarily mean perfect intellectual understanding. It is more a heart-knowing, and an acceptance of what is. It feels like being a droplet that re-enters the ocean and no longer has to struggle for survival, or to maintain an identity. It does not have to figure out where it is going, or the nature of its purpose. It just is.

Its boundaries have expanded and merged with the oneness. The single drop does not exist as before, and will never exist as that entity again. The atoms and molecules that comprised it do continue to exist, and may carry some memory of being that drop. They may emerge someday as part of another drop, or remain merged indefinitely.

If, when our souls took on physical form, we retained the memory, connection, and the *knowing* of the cosmic dance, we could relax and be fascinated by the kaleidoscope of experiences that come with earthly existence. Of course, we would do things much differently, because we would not be putting so much energy into the survival and control issues of ego.

We would not have the sense of separation that ego experiences, and we would realize that we are but many reflections of one soul. We would see there is no death, only transformation.

One of the reasons we may delight so much in butterflies is

because they show up unexpectedly, surprise us with their beauty, and then they are gone. We do not grieve the disappearance of the butterfly, for we know it is in its nature to fly away. We feel the same about rainbows and northern lights. We cannot own them, control them, or hold them. We can only marvel at them while they are here.

TRANSCENDING EGO

If we aligned with soul, we could feel this same sense of precious appreciation of other people, and even our own selves. We could delight in them (and ourselves) while we are here. If we acknowledged we are all just visiting, and could receive the call to return home at any time, our connections with one another would be even more precious.

We sometimes say we do not miss something until it is gone. A deeper statement might be that we do not truly appreciate things until we realize their impermanence. If that realization comes with their disappearance, it is a little late for that particular case. If we recognize and accept impermanence as a primary feature of our Universe, it is a little easier to let go. Perhaps we can learn to try not holding on so much in the first place.

It is very difficult for ego to grasp all of this. Remember in an earlier chapter, when I told the story of how my daughter, when only two, cried and cried when the sun went down? She was too young to understand the concept of the earth's spin. For her, it was a simple case of losing something to which she had become attached. All that could be done was to distract her from her pain, until her consciousness could hold what was really happening. So it is with ego. Soul would love to explain it all to the suffering ego, but ego simply cannot grasp it. This is not surprising, because the bottom line is that once we align with soul, there is not too much for ego to do.

Soul, however, does not give up. I realize here that I am personifying soul. It is more accurate to say the spirit of the Universe pulses through us, and is recognized as soul when we listen to it. It is easier to understand though, when we personify.

There are times when ego's boundaries crack, and that is when soul's presence can be felt in consciousness. Ego's boundaries may crack, or soften, in times of crisis, loss, transcendent experiences, meditative experiences, or surrender. Some of us seek connection with soul, and in effect become midwives in the birthing of our own soul awareness.

Others, for whom ego maintains a firm control, may never make the connection, or only find it in times of deep chaos or crisis. The crisis is often precipitated by the recognition that ego, in fact, has little or no control, beyond the confines of the illusory world it has created. The story comes crashing down when someone dies, a relationship ends, a job disappears, or physical illness changes one's life.

If, like the little boy who played king, we have built our world around a script, certain characters, and our role in that script, a major change feels like the end. It also feels as though now, there is nothing.

It may seem as though we have no purpose, no place, or identity. What we are feeling at that point is loss of ego. Still, soul is very present. It is as though the pain of that loss opens something deep within us. What seems heartbreaking may in fact be 'heart-awakening'.

If we go deep enough into the heart, through either pain or joy, we touch soul. Throughout the course of life, there will be many events that trigger an opening to soul. Like the chick whose outer shell is cracking, we can desperately try to hold things together, maintaining our safe little world, or let the shell of ego crumble, surrendering to something infinitely larger.

Each surrender is a mini-death. Each release from attachment, each acknowledgement of impermanence, prepares us for the soul's release of physical form. From soul's perspective, the transition from one form to another is as smooth and effortless as the transformation of water vapor. Nothing is lost: things have simply been rearranged.

How can this perspective assist us in our ego-based world, where, like it or not, we are attached to other people, and to our roles in each other's lives? Remember, we are evolving, and the shift from ego-based consciousness to soul-based consciousness is a transition in itself.

There is immeasurable value during this transition in releasing identification with our physical form. If we identify more with our souls, we can begin to feel a sense of our eternal nature, and see our experience on earth as only one brief moment in the larger, unfolding scheme. It is also helpful to tune in to the souls of others, to connect with them soul-to-soul. Soul connections are like having e-mail. With e-mail, you can stay connected with anyone virtually anywhere on the planet. With soul connections, you stay connected with other souls wherever either of you are in the Universe, in space, in time. Of course this does not necessarily mean that you hear them speak or see them. You feel them in your heart. A soul you have loved never ever leaves your heart. A mother who has miscarried may not even have seen the fetus, but she remains connected on a soul level with that being she carried, however briefly.

Our soul essence was never born, and it never dies. Soul essence has always been here. It is our physical form that was born. Through that physical form soul finds expression in the three-dimensional world. When the body dies, soul no longer expresses through that body, but it still exists.

If we have learned to connect on the level of soul, we do not need bodies! They are nice to have though, while we are in them, for they allow us to experience many earthly pleasures. However, they also substantiate the experience of pain, separation, sorrow, suffering, loneliness, and sadness. Bodies are not necessary to soul, but are more like earth-suits. Love does not require the presence of a body. We can love God, as God manifests in the physical world, but also in the non-physical manifestations. We can feel a deep loving connection with someone with whom we have had no physical contact in years. And certainly loved ones who have passed away live on in our hearts. We *know* this.

PHYSICAL DEATH

So why do we grieve death, even fear it? It is not the soul that does this. It is the ego. Ego will not get over it, and will wish for the one who has passed on to come back. Ego can no more understand the process than the two year old can understand why we cannot make the sun come back at night.

No matter how evolved we are, or how much we understand all of this, while on Earth, most of us will retain some remnants of ego. Consequently we will cry when loved ones die, and we will miss them when their physical form is no longer here. As we grow in soul consciousness however, we come to respect each soul's journey, and realize (unlike ego) that it is not just about us.

I remember when my dearly loved Grandmother died. I was heartbroken. As I stood crying on the steps of the church after the funeral, my cousin came to me and asked why I was crying. She said our grandmother lived a long, hard life, and it was her time to leave. I responded that I was not crying for her, I was crying for me!

A few years later that same beautiful cousin, whom I adored, died at the young age of thirty-seven. I love her as much today, and she is as alive in my heart as when she was here. It was hard to lose her, but I respected her journey.

I have worked with many couples who have lost children. A greater loss is hard to imagine. Such losses are a reminder to all that our children do not belong to us. In every case where a child has died, so many lives are touched. That child becomes a poignant teacher to all who hear of him or her, whether they knew the child or not. Perhaps that was his or her soul's purpose in this lifetime. It is so painful for the families, that, if we had the power, we might ask the child to adjust his or her soul's journey for our benefit. We cannot ask that of anyone.

I also believe if a soul is to be present in our lives, that soul will show up, one way or another. If a soul must move on, it will, no matter what. Parents who lose children spend endless hours trying to figure out something they could have done that might have prevented the child's death. They torture themselves, believing somehow they had the power to alter the path of another soul. Ego consciousness says: " It's my child, and I want it back!" Soul says: "I am so glad this special soul took on physical form long enough to touch my heart. I am changed forever, and now recognize my connection to the eternal."

Ego and soul also respond differently to the death of the physical body. If ego still perpetuates in consciousness the belief that earthly existence is all there is, and that leaving earth means losing everything, naturally the prospect of death is traumatic.

Soul consciousness brings comfort and acceptance. Perhaps Shakespeare was right, and "all the world's a stage". When the curtain comes down, the play is over. Then we can go back to what is real, eliminating the costumes, masks, make-up and roles.

METAMORPHOSIS

Soul does not exist *within* the body: it expresses *through* it. Where then does soul reside? Soul is everywhere. It may be only a glimpse of soul that shines through physical form. When we die, we may well connect with the larger soul of all, even with those who are still living. We merge and become one. There is no greater intimacy and connection than that. Just as a bird must leave the tree in order to fly, soul one day no longer needs to express through our physical form. Imagine soul as a butterfly, and the body as the cocoon. It makes little sense to grieve for the loss of the cocoon. If we did not understand what happened, or did not see that a butterfly emerged, we may only feel loss. Once we understand the process, there is joy and delight. A metamorphosis has occurred. There has been a transcendence. The dance continues.

EXERCISES:

Think of someone you love who has passed on. Close your eyes, and feel that person in your heart. Allow your heart to open as the love you feel expands.

1) Think of others who have died. What learnings did you gain from the life of each?
2) What learnings did you gain from their deaths?
3) Imagine you have left the earth, and are pure soul. Look back on all with whom you shared your journey. What is it you would have liked to have told them before you left?
4) Write out the messages you would have wanted to give to others. Plan to communicate those messages within the next few days, either verbally, or in writing.

The Ultimate Letting Go

5) Ask yourself what your ego is attached to in this lifetime. Imagine letting go.
6) Write your epitaph.
7) Now, go live it.

Chapter 12

FULL CIRCLE

Throughout these pages we have traced the development of human consciousness from pure soul of the newborn, through the development of ego, the shift to more soulful consciousness, and ultimately to the final release of ego and the transition back to pure soul.

We have come full circle, but what a journey in between! I am reminded of the Disney movie, *Jumanji*. It is about children who find a board game, buried, but revealed due to an excavation. They dig it out and decide to play it, having no idea what they are getting into. They shake the dice and move around the board. Each space they land upon takes them into a completely different experience, a different reality, and a different era. While they are in that experience, it becomes their whole world. They lose any remembrance of the game they are playing, and become completely caught up in the drama of each situation. Once they have moved all the way around the board, the game is over. All of the experiences swirl around like water going down a drain, and disappear back into the game board, leaving it fresh and empty, as it was in the beginning. We know the game may be hidden away again, but one day it will be found by other children, years or eons later, who will play the game, going through their own series of experiences, depending where they land on the board.

SOUL'S EXPERIENCE ON EARTH

This story made me think about soul's experience on Earth. Soul takes on physical form and the accompanying ego consciousness, then experiences unfold according to where that soul has 'landed'—where in time, where in space, which geographical location, and in what life context. Other dimensions to soul's experience include gender, relationship to other souls (child, spouse, friend, enemy, teacher, boss), and soul's purpose.

There are many layers in consciousness, some that lie beyond our identity or 'beingness'. Imagine again, concentric circles of awareness. The innermost relate to physical form and ego awareness. This is the 'me' aspect. The outermost circles transcend physicality, or beingness. They are the aspects that merge back into the Oneness. There is no 'me', no 'being', but simply an eternal 'is-ness'.

SOUL TAKES FLIGHT

Think of the first humans who envisioned being able to fly. They had to figure out how to create the energies that would allow a physically heavy machine to remain aloft in thin air. Our species is in a similar place now. We are trying to figure out how to allow our souls to take flight while still 'connected' to a dense, heavy physical form. To some, it seems impossible. But many never believed those 'strange flying machines' would ever get off the ground either.

The energies that will provide the 'lift' enabling us to transcend our older, earth-based, physical perspectives are the energies of soulful love. It will be our open-hearted connections with others, our 'seeing' through the eyes of soulful love and into the heart of all things, that will raise us to new levels of being. Does this mean giving up ego altogether?

Well, no: ego is, for now, an inherent part of our humanness. If you are an enlightened master, or you are living your life in meditation on a mountaintop, then it becomes easier to drop ego. You would not be constantly triggered by the egos of others, and you do not really have relationships with others in the traditional sense. You can 'be' pure spirit, because you are living almost completely in a world centered on spirit. Most of us do not live in that world, so we have to deal with traffic, bills, employers, and relatives.

The purpose of this book has been to assist you to bring the more soulful aspects of your being into the real world of your own experience. On an individual level, it has been shown that doing so results in better health, more fulfilling relationships, and a more meaningful life. In a more esoteric sense, it could be said that soulful living is a way to experience heaven on earth. It certainly allows access to the highest qualities of our humanness.

On a more global level, the issue is survival of the species. Interestingly, more species have become extinct than have survived and evolved. We have a choice between rendering ourselves extinct, or participating in the emergence of more highly evolved beings. In the past, the evolutionary advantage was with the physically strongest, fastest, most able to survive predators, and the elements. It was a physical thing. Now that we have used our minds to develop means of protection and survival that do not depend on our own physical capabilities, (most of us, in the Western world, don't have to hunt and gather big — businesses take care of that), the playing field is no longer at a physical level. It is now at the level of mind.

CONSCIOUS EVOLUTION

As noted earlier, in humans, for the first time, a species can consciously participate in its own evolution. The human mind collectively can make choices that contribute to our ultimate extinction, or it can co-create an evolution to a higher stage of development. As Jonas Salk suggested, in order for nature to protect and preserve its magnificent creation, the tendency certainly would be to favor and select those human minds that would have the power to correct inherent destructive tendencies in mankind, and therefore to become dominant forces for the continuation of human evolution.

The capacity exists, within the human mind, to respond in ways that support fulfillment of evolutionary potential. The choice we have is whether to activate it or not: whether to shape and orient our minds and the minds of our children to make choices that are pro-evolutionary. If evolution were an Olympic event, you can be sure there would be training centers around the world, and many countries would have a national team to set the pace.

However, evolution is no longer about competition. If anything, it is a team sport, and we are all on the same team. The more we develop our own skills, as well as encouraging and supporting everyone else, the better we, and those following us, will fare.

More than ever, the world needs the thoughts of those human minds that point the way forward along the evolutionary path. When your heart and mind are open, and you allow those thoughts to resonate with that place deep within your soul that holds the same knowing, cosmic intelligence is amplified. Rather than remaining as implicate potential, it becomes a very real force in our lives, and carries us forward and upward towards our highest selves.

Soul learns to take flight within our own being. When that happens, ego and personality are lifted as well. Like booster rockets, one day they will drop away, as they will no longer be required.

In the meantime, the view is breathtaking, the experience deeper and richer than anything before. It is a once-in-a-lifetime event: one that for both micro- and macro-cosmic reasons ought not to be missed.

ISBN 1412014042-2